FOREIGN CAPITAL, SAVINGS AND GROWTH

INTERNATIONAL STUDIES IN ECONOMICS AND ECONOMETRICS

VOLUME 9

FOREIGN CAPITAL, SAVINGS AND GROWTH

An International Cross-Section Study

by

KANHAYA L. GUPTA

University of Alberta, Edmonton, Alberta, Canada

and

M. ANISUL ISLAM

University of Dacca, Bangladesh

D. REIDEL PUBLISHING COMPANY

DORDRECHT-HOLLAND / BOSTON-U.S.A.

Library of Congress Cataloging in Publication Data

Gupta, Kanhaya L. (Kanhaya Lal), 1935–
Foreign capital, savings, and growth.

(International studies in economics and econometrics ; v. 9)
Bibliography: p.
Includes index.
1. Underdeveloped areas–Investments, Foreign–Mathematical models. 2. Underdeveloped areas–Saving and investment–Mathematical models. 3. Underdeveloped areas–Mathematical models. I. Islam, M. Anisul, 1952– . II. Title. III. Series.
HG5993.G86 1983 332.6′73′091724 82-23146
ISBN-13: 978-94-009-7887-4 e-ISBN-13: 978-94-009-7885-0
DOI:10.1007/978-94-009-7885-0

Published by D. Reidel Publishing Company,
P.O. Box 17, 3300 AA Dordrecht, Holland.

Sold and distributed in the U.S.A. and Canada
by Kluwer Boston Inc.,
190 Old Derby Street, Hingham, MA 02043, U.S.A.

In all other countries, sold and distributed
by Kluwer Academic Publishers Group,
P.O. Box 322, 3300 AH Dordrecht, Holland.

D. Reidel Publishing Company is a member of the Kluwer Group.

Softcover reprint of the hardcover 1st Edition 1983

To Karuna, Jonathan
and
the Late Momena Akhtar Begum

TABLE OF CONTENTS

ACKNOWLEDGEMENTS

We would like to thank Alan Sharpe for his excellent computational assistance, to Charlene Hill for her careful job of typing several drafts of the manuscript and to the reader of the D. Reidel Publishing Company for his very painstaking and careful comments which improved the exposition considerably.

We are grateful to the following for permission to reproduce copyright material:

Frank Cass & Co. Ltd. for the extract from K. L. Gupta's 'Foreign Capital Inflows and Output Growth Rate: A Reformulation', *Journal of Development Studies* **XIII** (October, 1976); the Publishers of *Kyklos* for tables and extracts from K. L. Gupta's 'Foreign Capital Inflows, Dependency Burden and Savings Rates in Developing Countries: A Simultaneous Equation Model', *Kyklos* 28 (1975); Longman Inc., and author Michael P. Todaro for Tables 14.2. and 14.5. from *Economic Development in the Third World*, 2nd Edition, 1981; and Pergamon Press, Inc., for 'World Development Report 1979, Annex Table 16'.

LIST OF TABLES

Table

TABLES IN THE APPENDIX C

Table

CHAPTER I

INTRODUCTION

The growing disparity between the developed and the developing countries has once again rekindled the debate about the relative merits of foreign investment as means whereby the developed countries can help the developing countries in both achieving a reasonable rate of growth and also from preventing the widening gap between the North and the South from widening even further. This renewed interest in the debate was most sharply highlighted at the recently concluded North–South economic summit conference at Cancun, Mexico. There, the United States took the position that massive increases in foreign aid were neither practical nor the best means of ensuring continuing and satisfactory growth in the developing countries. Rather the solution was to be found in depending on a free market economy and on inflows of private foreign investment. Behind these views, of course lie the more fundamental questions: for example, what should be the role of multinational corporations in the developing countries since they constitute the main source of foreign private investment? Should there be greater cooperation between the public sectors of the North and the South? What is the best means of bridging the economic gap between the North and the South: through direct transfers of wealth from the North to the South or through raising South's growth rates via the transfer of technology and the inflow of investment by multinationals? These questions are of fundamental importance and have wide ranging implications, not only for the economic questions under consideration but also for the social and political well being of the developing countries and, in fact, for the world at large. However, there is an important narrower question, which is of immediate concern and which has implications for the debate. This relates to the quantitative significance of domestic resources via-à-vis that of all foreign capital inflows on the one hand and of different component's of foreign capital inflows on the other. In other words, which is more beneficial to the developing countries: Foreign aid or private foreign investment? In this study, we wish to address ourselves to this narrowly defined question.

There have been some efforts in the literature in providing quantitative answers to this question.[1] Most of these studies have concentrated upon examining the impact of foreign inflows on savings and on the rate of growth of the developing countries. The common approach has been to specify some kind of single equation models for savings and for growth rates and include foreign capital inflows, either in their aggregate form or in a somewhat disaggregated form among the determinants of these two variables.

This approach, while useful as a first approximation, is rather deficient in the sense that, by now we have a substantial body of literature, both theoretical and empirical, to suggest that savings and growth rates affect each other. This means that for a proper appreciation of the quantitative magnitudes of the effect of foreign capital inflows, we must allow for this simultaneity. Single equation models ignore this simultaneity.

The aim of this book, therefore, is to specify and estimate a simultaneous equation model in which savings and growth will be jointly determined. However, before we do this, we will also present new estimates based on single equation models. Our rationale for presenting these results, despite our reservations about single equation models, is based on three factors. First, most of the single equation studies have covered time periods for the 1950s and the 1960s. Therefore, it will be interesting to see as to what extent the effects of foreign capital inflows have changed over time even using simple framework. Second, we will present a model of economic growth which we believe to be more sophisticated than the existing single equation models used for this purpose. And finally, for both savings and growth rates, we will present far more disaggregated results than ever presented before.

The scheme of the book is as follows. Chapter II briefly presents some descriptive material on variables of interest for this study and looks at changes in them over the past few decades. In Chapter III, we first present a brief review and critique of existing single equation models on the determinants of the rate of growth in developing countries. We then present our own model and its estimates for a group of fifty two developing countries using data for early 1970s. Chapter IV carries out a somewhat similar exercise for the determinants of savings. In Chapter V, we examine the implications of using a simultaneous equations framework. Chapter VI is devoted to the specification and estimation of a simultaneous equation model. In Chapter VII, we perform multiplier analysis using the estimates obtained in Chapter VI and compare them with the results derived from the single equation models of Chapters III and IV. Chapter VIII concerns itself with the problem of intertemporal stability of the various relationships. In Chapter IX, we examine the usefulness of the single and the simultaneous equation models as predictive tools and as indicators for the relative performance of various countries. In the final chapter we summarize our main findings and point out avenues for further research. The details of the data are provided in Appendixes A and B. The reduced form equations and the elasticity multiplier tables are given in Appendix C.

CHAPTER II

FOREIGN CAPITAL, SAVINGS AND GROWTH: SOME DESCRIPTIVE INDICATORS

As a preliminary to the quantitative analysis presented in the subsequent chapters, we present in this chapter some summary data on the behaviour of growth rates, savings rates, per capita income and foreign capital inflows for different time periods and for various subgroupings. The aim is to see what kinds of different behavioural patterns are represented by the different categories. Mere casual observation of the data sometimes can throw interesting light on causal relationships between different variables. It would, in this case, be interesting to see whether there have been any significant changes in any of these variables over time and/or between different income and geographical groups. In Section 1, we present some analysis of the trend, pattern and sources of different types of capital inflows in general. In Section 2, we present some summary statistics of our sample data for different time periods and sample groups. In Section 3, we attempt some further interpretations of the summary statistics.

1. TRENDS, PATTERNS AND SOURCES OF DIFFERENT TYPES OF FOREIGN CAPITAL INFLOWS

Since the major emphasis of the present study is to analyze the impact of foreign capital inflows on the behaviour of growth and savings in the developing countries, it is of great interest to observe the trends and patterns of different types of foreign capital inflows as a preliminary to further analysis. In Table II.1, we have reported the dollar amount of different types of capital inflows from 1965 to 1979. We observe that the volume of total capital inflow has increased by 593% [from $10 668 million in 1965–67 to $73 943 million from 1965 to 1979]. During this period, foreign aid, as a major component of total capital inflow, has only increased by 283%. This indicates that foreign private investment, another major component, has been increasing at a much faster rate than foreign aid. This is clearly seen from rows E and F of Table I. Here we find that foreign aid as a percentage of total capital flow has declined from 61.2% to only 33.9% during this period while foreign private investment has increased its share from 38.8% to 66.1%. Given this relative growth of foreign private investment, it will be of interest to

TABLE II.1.
Net flow of different types of foreign capital from developed to developing countries: 1965–1979 (million dollars)

Source and type	1967	1965–1970 Average	1975	1976	1977	1978	1979[a]
A. Foreign aid	6533.1	7929.2	16608.7	16970.7	18014.8	25035.8	25031.7
Official Development Assistance (ODA)	6118.0	6790.5	13585.1	13665.4	14695.7	19986.0	22375.4
Bilateral	5642.6	5666.7	9815.3	9504.6	10083.7	13123.4	15913.8
Grants and grantlike contributions	3656.2	3309.2	6268.0	6541.9	7202.7	9402.8	11285.5
Development lending and capital	1986.3	2357.4	3547.1	2962.1	2881.1	3720.6	4628.4
Contributions to multilateral institutions	475.4	1123.8	3769.6	4160.9	4611.9	6862.6	6461.4
Grants	223.7	540.6	1731.6	2166.5	2338.1	2416.7	3435.4
Capital subscription payments	10.9	31.5	9.5	61.4	38.8	184.4	88.5
Other offical flows	415.1	1138.7	3023.6	3305.3	3319.1	5049.8	2656.3
B. Foreign private investment	4134.8	6875.1	22427.0	22417.0	28190.9	44325.4	46965.4
Private investment and lending	3174.0	4733.2	18285.6	16993.2	20141.5	34351.0	37542.2
Private export credits	960.8	2141.9	4141.9	5423.8	8049.3	9974.4	9423.2
C. Grants by private voluntary agencies	n.a.	857.5	1341.8	1354.5	1488.8	1675.7	1946.3
D. Total	10667.9	15661.8	40378.1	40742.2	47694.7	71036.6	73943.3
E. Foreign aid as % of total	61.2	50.6	41.1	41.7	37.8	35.2	33.9
F. Private investment as % of total	38.8	49.4	58.9	58.3	62.2	64.8	66.1

Sources: M.P.Todaro: *Economic Development in the Third World*, 2nd ed. (Longman Inc., New York, 1981), p.409; *Development Cooperation, 1977 Review* (OECD, Paris, 1977), p. 188; and *Development Cooperation*, 1978 Review (Preliminary) (OECD, Paris, 1978), Table A-19; *Development Cooperation*, 1980 Review (OECD, Paris, 1980), Table A-16.

[a] 1979 data are preliminary estimates.

analyze the relative effectiveness of different types of foreign capital inflows on the economic development of the recipient countries. This question will be pursued in more detail in later chapters.

One related question is to ask why foreign private investment was growing at a much faster rate than foreign aid? Two major reasons can be put forward. First, the rapid growth of the multinational corporations and their interests in world wide operations,[1] which led to the enormous increase in the volume of foreign private investment in the developing countries. Second, the volume of foreign aid was not increasing rapidly enough because the flows of foreign aid (as a percent of GNP) from major donor countries were in fact declining. This phenomenon can be observed from Table II.2. which reports the flow of

TABLE II.2.
Net flow of foreign aid as percentage of donor country's GNP: 1960–1981

Donor country	% of donor country GNP									
	1960	1965	1970	1975	1976	1977	1978	1979	1980[a]	1981[a]
Australia	0.38	0.53	0.59	0.60	0.42	0.45	0.45	0.45	0.47	0.47
Austria	–	0.11	0.07	0.17	0.12	0.24	0.28	0.28	0.29	0.29
Belgium	0.88	0.60	0.46	0.59	0.51	0.46	0.52	0.54	0.56	0.59
Canada	0.19	0.19	0.42	0.55	0.46	0.50	0.52	0.49	0.50	0.50
Denmark	0.09	0.13	0.38	0.58	0.56	0.60	0.75	0.70	0.73	0.76
France	1.38	0.76	0.66	0.62	0.62	0.60	0.57	0.60	0.60	0.61
Germany	0.31	0.40	0.32	0.40	0.31	0.27	0.31	0.33	0.33	0.33
Italy	0.22	0.10	0.16	0.11	0.13	0.10	0.08	0.09	0.09	0.08
Japan	0.24	0.27	0.23	0.23	0.20	0.21	0.23	0.24	0.25	0.26
Netherlands	0.31	0.36	0.61	0.75	0.82	0.85	0.82	0.91	0.96	0.99
New Zealand	–	–	0.23	0.52	0.41	0.39	0.34	0.35	0.34	0.35
Norway	0.11	0.16	0.32	0.66	0.70	0.82	0.90	0.98	0.99	1.00
Portugal	1.45	0.59	0.67	0.70	–	–	–	–	–	–
Sweden	0.05	0.19	0.38	0.82	0.82	0.99	0.88	0.96	0.99	0.99
Switzerland	0.04	0.09	0.15	0.19	0.19	0.19	0.20	0.21	0.21	0.22
United Kingdom	0.56	0.47	0.36	0.37	0.38	0.37	0.40	0.41	0.42	0.43
United States	0.53	0.49	0.31	0.26	0.25	0.22	0.23	0.22	0.22	0.22
Average: of the countries above	0.45	0.34	0.37	0.48	0.43	0.45	0.47	0.49	0.50	0.51
Foreign aid as % of GNP of countries above	0.51	0.45	0.34	0.35	0.33	0.31	0.32	0.33	0.34	0.34

Source: M.P. Todaro, *op. cit*., p. 410, *World Development Report*, 1979, Annex Table 16.
[a] Preliminary estimates.

foreign aid (as % of donor country's GNP) by the major donor countries from 1960 to 1981. In Table II.2., we find that the average ratio for all donor countries has increased from 0.45% in 1960 to 0.51% in 1981. But the average data do not provide an accurate pattern of the flow of foreign aid. It is mainly because, except for some small donor countries like Austria, Australia, Canada, Denmark, etc., this ratio has been declining steadily and rapidly for the major aid donor countries like France, Germany, Japan, United Kingdom, and the United States. This average was biased upward due to the increase in the ratio for countries like the Netherlands, Norway, Sweden, etc., for whom it rose very rapidly towards 1.0% of GNP. A more accurate picture is represented by the last row of the table which gives the ratio of total foreign aid of all the donor countries as a percentage of the donor country's total GNP. We observe that this ratio has steadily declined from 0.51% in 1960 to 0.34% in 1981.

In Table II.3., we present some data on the flow of foreign aid from different multilateral institutions. In this table, figures in the brackets refer to the relevant percentages of the total multilateral aid flow. From this table, we observe the following: (i) Total multilateral aid has increased by 479% from 1970 to 1976 (From $1784 million in 1970 to $10324 million in 1979.) (ii) Multilateral aid from World Bank group has increased more rapidly than from other sources such as the United Nations. In fact, as a % of total multilateral flow, the flow from the United Nations, Regional banks and European Communities has declined considerably. (iii) Most of the concessional loans come from United Nations sources. (iv) Aid from the OPEC and Arab institutions is increasing rapidly but their percentage is still very small (only 15% of the total in 1978).

2. SUMMARY STATISTICS OF SAMPLE DATA ON GROWTH, SAVINGS, INCOME AND CAPITAL INFLOWS

In this section, we present some summary statistics of our sample data for two time periods and different subgroups. The data on average growth rates of GNP and savings rates are presented for two time periods: 1950–1960 and 1965–1973 in Tables II.4. and II.5., respectively. The data on foreign capital inflows are given both in aggregative form and in terms of three components, namely, foreign aid, foreign private investment and other inflows.[2] This breakdown is adopted by the World Bank. But even apart from this, the significance of such a disaggregation is obvious given the fact that the three types of inflows are often determined by different factors and have different

TABLE II.3.
Net flow of foreign capital from multilateral institutions to developing countries, 1970–1979 (million dollars)

Institutions	Concessional							Total						
	1970	1974	1975	1976	1977	1978	1979	1970	1974	1975	1976	1977	1978	1979
World Bank Group	163	901	1026	1326	1171	1083	1385	739	2247	3064	3243	3063	3254	4339
(% of total)	(14.9)	(31.6)	(28.3)	(34.3)	(23.6)	(18.1)	(22.6)	(41.4)	(48.3)	(47.7)	(49.1)	(38.9)	(34.5)	(42.0)
United Nations	498	939	1457	1252	1404	1711	2000	498	939	1457	1252	1404	1711	2000
(% of total)	(45.4)	(33.0)	(38.0)	(32.3)	(28.3)	(28.5)	(32.7)	(27.9)	(20.2)	(22.7)	(20.0)	(17.8)	(18.2)	(19.4)
Regional Banks[a]	225	293	413	369	434	552	531	326	708	936	936	1124	1239	1355
(% of total)	(20.5)	(10.3)	(10.8)	(9.5)	(8.7)	(9.2)	(8.7)	(18.3)	(15.2)	(14.6)	(14.2)	(14.3)	(13.2)	(13.1)
European Communities	210	598	721	501	539	805	1257	221	614	748	559	598	883	1419
(% of total)	(19.2)	(21.0)	(18.9)	(12.9)	(11.1)	(13.4)	(20.5)	(12.4)	(13.2)	(14.6)	(8.5)	(7.6)	(9.4)	(13.7)
OPEC and Arab Institutions[b]	–	116	160	423	1232	966	271	–	140	216	609	1496	1446	–
(% of total)	–	(4.1)	(4.2)	(10.9)	(24.8)	(16.1)	(4.4)	–	(3.0)	(3.4)	(9.2)	(19.0)	(15.4)	–
Total	1096	2847	3837	3871	4965	5995	6124	1784	4648	6421	6599	7870	9402	10 324

Notes: [a] This group includes Inter-American Development Bank, Asian Development Bank and African Development Bank. [b] Gulf organization for Development of Egypt, Arab fund for Economic and Social Development and Special Arab Fund for Africa. [c] Preliminary estimates.

Sources: M. P. Todaro, *Ibid*., p. 412; *Development Cooperation 1977 Review* (OECD, Paris, 1977), pp. 65 and 197; and *Development Cooperation, 1978 Review* (Preliminary) (OECD, Paris, 1978), Table G-3; *Development Cooperation, 1980 Review* (OECD, Paris, 1980), Table C-2.

TABLE II.4.[a]
Comparison of average growth rates of GNP between different time periods and different sample groups

	1950–1960		1965–1973	
	Mean growth rate (%)	Standard deviation of growth rate	Mean growth rate (%)	Standard deviation of growth rate
A. *40 Country Sample*				
(i) *All 40 Countries*	5.02	2.27	5.97	2.07
(ii) *Income Groups*:				
Group I	4.07	2.17	4.33	2.23
Group II	4.65	1.36	6.07	2.16
Group III	5.86	2.56	6.55	2.48
(iii) *Regional Groups*:				
Asia	6.45	1.99	7.02	2.74
Africa	3.56	1.99	4.88	2.70
Latin America	4.63	2.01	5.34	1.81
B. *52 Country Sample*				
(i) *All 52 Countries*	–	–	5.91	2.48
(ii) *Income Groups*:				
Group I	–	–	4.44	2.01
Group II	–	–	6.19	1.98
Group III	–	–	6.73	2.67
(iii) *Regional Groups*:				
Asia	–	–	7.03	2.85
Africa	–	–	4.92	2.46
Latin America	–	–	5.27	1.80

[a] *Source*: Calculated from *World Tables*, Johns Hopkins University Press, Baltimore, 1976. See also the Appendixes to this book.

characteristics. Be that as it may, the four flows are given in Tables II.6. to II.9. All of the four are expressed as proportions of GNP – in percentage terms. The data on the growth rate, and the savings rate, again in percentage terms – are given in the first two tables. The data on per capita income, in U.S. dollars, are given in Table II.10.

In all cases, we have presented the data both for the total sample and for two sub-groupings. The rationale for these groupings is given in the later

TABLE II.5.[a]
Comparison of savings rates between different time periods and different sample groups

	1950–1960		1965–1973	
	Mean savings rate (%)	Standard deviation of savings rate	Mean savings rate (%)	Standard deviation of savings rate
A. *40 Country Sample*				
(i) *All 40 Countries*	13.51	5.95	16.13	5.63
(ii) *Income Groups*:				
Group I	9.81	6.17	12.45	5.42
Group II	13.12	3.41	13.81	3.04
Group III	16.00	6.13	18.45	6.95
(iii) *Regional Groups*				
Asia	13.57	6.30	17.16	8.06
Africa	11.23	7.04	12.68	6.19
Latin America	14.35	4.90	15.24	3.72
B. *52 Country Sample*				
(i) *All 52 Countries*	–	–	15.97	6.52
(ii) *Income Groups*:				
Group I	–	–	12.41	5.64
Group II	–	–	15.44	4.70
Group III	–	–	18.92	6.90
(iii) *Regional Groups*:				
Asia	–	–	17.19	8.53
Africa	–	–	13.98	7.05
Latin America	–	–	15.44	3.75

[a] *Source*: See Table II.4.

chapters. We do, however, need to explain the selection of two different sample sizes. The reason for the first sample, forty countries, was that it was the maximum number of countries for which we could find consistent data for the two time periods on the relevant variables. The size of the second sample was dictated, once again, by the availability factor. Since our quantitative analysis is based on the latest available data, we wanted to have as large a sample as possible and fifty two was the maximum number of countries for which we could find all of the pertinent information.

TABLE II.6.[a]
Comparison of the rate of foreign capital inflow (as percentage of GNP) between different time periods and different sample groups

	1950–1960		1965–1973	
	Mean rate of total capital inflow (%)	Standard deviation	Mean rate of total capital inflow (%)	Standard deviation
A. *40 Country Sample*				
(i) *All 40 Countries*	1.99	2.46	4.42	3.63
(ii) *Income Groups*:				
Group I	1.28	0.89	2.78	1.61
Group II	2.39	3.17	5.41	3.01
Group III	2.11	2.36	4.13	4.33
(iii) *Regional Groups*:				
Asia	1.34	1.72	3.36	3.78
Africa	1.26	0.97	4.39	2.88
Latin America	2.72	3.04	4.67	3.43
B. *52 Country Sample*				
(i) *All 52 Countries*	–	–	3.93	3.45
(ii) *Income Groups*:				
Group I	–	–	3.04	–
Group II	–	–	4.84	–
Group III	–	–	3.86	–
(iii) *Regional Groups*:				
Asia	–	–	3.29	–
Africa	–	–	4.09	–
Latin America	–	–	4.37	–

[a] *Source*: See Table II.4.

The data on per capita income are given for three time periods: 1955, 1970 and 1973.

In each of the first seven tables, we have also given the standard deviation of the variables. This helps us to make careful statements about the significence of the observed differences, whether over time, inter-group or intragroup.

In Table II.4., average growth rate of GNP and their respective standard deviations have been reported for the aggregate sample as well as for different income and geographic groups [3] for two time periods. We observe the following: (i) In terms of intertemporal behaviour, we observe remarkable stability of the mean growth rate for the 40 countries over the two time periods, that is, the mean growth rate has increased only slightly from 5.02% to 5.97% with standard deviations remaining almost the same. (ii) In terms of income groups, income groups I and III displayed stable behaviour, while the income group II shows remarkable dynamism in terms of growth performance. For this group, the mean growth rate has increased from 4.65% to 6.07% per annum but the standard deviation has also increased from 1.36 to 2.16 which indicates that some countries within this group were growing at a much faster rate than other countries in the group. (iii) In come group I was experiencing a very low rate of growth compared to the other two groups. This pattern is more prominent during the latter period than the earlier period, that is, the second group was catching up with the third income group while the first income group was lagging behind. (iv) Looking at the geographical disaggregation, we find that, on the average, countries in Asia were experiencing a higher growth rate in both periods compared to countries in Africa and Latin America.

It is interesting to note that the behaviour of savings rate (see Table II.5.) is not similar to that of growth rate described earlier. For the 40 countries, the savings rate has increased by 3 percentage points, but in terms of income groups, the maximum gain was experienced by the first and the third income groups. Unlike the experience with respect to growth, the savings rate in the second income group remained virtually the same. Of course, in terms of geographical groups, the pattern is similar to that of growth, namely, on an average, countries in Asia had a higher savings rate in both time periods than countries in Africa and Latin America.

We now turn to the analysis of the behaviour of the foreign capital inflows in aggregative form in Table II.6. Each entry in this table represents the ratio of foreign capital inflow to recipient country's GNP, on average, in percentage terms. For the 40 countries, this ratio has increased from 1.99% in 1950–60 to 4.42% in 1965–73 indicating an increasing role of foreign capital in the management of the domestic economies in the recipient countries. As a percentage of GNP, the flow of aggregate foreign capital has increased during these two periods for all income groups and all geographical groups. But the relative rate of increase has been different for different groups. For example, maximum increase has been experienced by the countries in income group II and the sample countries in Africa. In terms of inter-group comparisons, we also observe that in both time periods, this ratio was higher for income group

II relative to income groups I and III. In geographical groups, of course, the ratio is higher for Latin America than for Asia and Africa.

The average behaviour of aggregate foreign capital described above does not hold when analysis is carried out in terms of its components, that is, foreign aid (Table II.7.), foreign private investment (Table II.8.), and other inflows (Table II.9.). We still observe that, for both time periods, and for both foreign aid and foreign private investment, this ratio was higher for income group II compared to the other two groups, which is also consistent

TABLE II.7.[a]
Comparison of the average ratio of foreign aid to GNP between different time periods and different sample groups

	1950–1960		1965–1973	
	Average ratio of aid to GNP (%)	Standard deviation	Average ratio of aid to GNP (%)	Standard deviation
A. *40 Country Sample*				
(i) *All 40 Countries*	1.09	1.82	2.06	2.43
(ii) *Income Groups*:				
Group I	1.09	1.02	3.09	3.99
Group II	1.61	1.29	2.16	1.12
Group III	0.70	2.35	1.79	1.90
(iii) *Regional Groups*:				
Asia	1.14	1.50	3.28	1.83
Africa	0.54	1.23	1.70	1.52
Latin America	1.53	1.19	2.44	3.02
B. *52 Country Sample*				
(i) *All 52 Countries*	–	–	2.12	2.31
(ii) *Income Groups*:				
Group I	–	–	2.72	3.33
Group II	–	–	2.31	1.39
Group III	–	–	1.55	1.80
(iii) *Regional Groups*:				
Asia	–	–	1.87	1.73
Africa	–	–	2.29	1.72
Latin America	–	–	2.33	2.99

[a] *Source*: See Table II.4.

TABLE II.8.[a]
Comparison of the average ratio of foreign private investment to GNP between different time periods and different sample groups

	1950–1960		1965–1973	
	Average ratio of *FPI* to GNP (%)	Standard deviation	Average ratio of *FPI* to GNP (%)	Standard deviation
A. *40 Country Sample*				
(i) *All 40 Countries*	0.80	1.48	1.27	2.85
(ii) *Income Groups*:				
Group I	0.35	0.53	−0.58	2.95
Group II	0.53	1.46	1.61	1.44
Group III	1.28	1.71	1.57	3.29
(iii) *Regional Groups*:				
Asia	0.52	0.66	0.29	0.97
Africa	1.63	2.33	1.34	1.60
Latin America	0.70	1.27	1.42	3.81
B. *52 Country Sample*				
(i) *All 52 Countries*	–	–	1.03	2.59
(ii) *Income Groups*:				
Group I	–	–	−0.12	2.57
Group II	–	–	1.49	1.36
Group III	–	–	1.51	3.03
(iii) *Regional Groups*:				
Asia	–	–	0.43	1.16
Africa	–	–	1.27	1.57
Latin America	–	–	1.40	3.72

[a] *Source*: See Table II.4.

with observed patterns of aggregate capital inflows. But when it comes to relative increase over the two time periods, the pattern seems to be quite different for different types of capital inflows. For example, as a percentage of GNP, the maximum increase is experienced by Group I and Asia in terms of foreign aid whereas in terms of foreign private investment the maximum increase is observed by countries in Income Group II and Latin America over the two time periods. In terms of foreign private investment, this ratio, in fact, has been declining for countries in income group I and Asia.

TABLE II.9.[a]
Comparison of the average ratio of other capital inflows to GNP between different time periods and different sample groups

	1950–1960		1965–1973	
	Average of the ratio of other inflows to GNP (%)	Standard deviation	Average of the ratio of other inflows to GNP (%)	Standard deviation
A. *40 Country Sample*				
(i) *All 40 Countries*	0.10	2.18	1.09	2.29
(ii) *Income Groups*:				
Group I	–0.16	0.93	0.27	1.74
Group II	0.25	2.87	1.64	1.49
Group III	0.14	2.07	0.77	2.83
(iii) *Regional Groups*:				
Asia	–0.32	0.79	0.80	2.81
Africa	–0.32	2.12	1.36	2.09
Latin America	0.49	2.67	0.82	1.84
B. *52 Country Sample*				
(i) *All 52 Countries*	–	–	0.77	2.27
(ii) *Income Groups*:				
Group I	–	–	0.44	1.46
Group II	–	–	1.04	1.91
Group III	–	–	0.80	2.89
(iii) *Regional Groups*:				
Asia	–	–	0.99	2.69
Africa	–	–	0.53	2.32
Latin America	–	–	0.64	1.96

[a] *Source*: See Table II.4.

The above analysis has shed some important light in understanding the pattern of average behaviour of different variables over time and between different income and regional groups of countries. The analysis also indicates some a priori relationships between different variables such as growth, savings and different types of capital inflows. We will discuss these relationships in observed data in more detail in the next section. The previous discussion has also highlighted the importance of disaggregation not only of the sample countries into income and geographic groups, but also of the disaggregation of variables such as foreign capital into its various components.

TABLE II.10.[a]
Comparison of average per capita income between different time periods and different sample groups

	1955		1970		1973	
	Average per capita income U.S. ($)	Standard deviation	Average per capita income U.S. ($)	Standard deviation	Average per capita income U.S. ($)	Standard deviation
A. *40 Country Sample*						
(i) *All 40 Countries*	242.95	156.43	527.46	397.15	815.20	745.63
(ii) *Income Groups*:						
Group I	94.10	28.82	133.30	57.88	168.00	75.74
Group II	195.54	41.08	319.92	62.06	457.69	120.20
Group III	366.77	160.37	633.53	398.03	1381.18	807.81
(iii) *Regional Groups*:						
Asia	170.62	165.11	442.23	571.22	806.15	1109.60
Africa	209.75	116.40	533.13	368.15	875.00	677.22
Latin America	298.05	148.82	493.90	237.49	696.50	381.70
B. *52 Country Sample*						
(i) *All 52 Countries*	–	–	460.87	377.89	738.27	706.11
(ii) *Income Groups*:						
Group I	–	–	128.93	59.04	164.00	76.66
Group II	–	–	320.38	56.61	466.88	116.66
Group III	–	–	805.00	369.48	1355.24	740.07
(iii) *Regional Groups*:						
Asia	–	–	448.39	503.86	841.67	990.04
Africa	–	–	231.00	169.16	335.00	280.33
Latin America	–	–	510.00	242.69	709.52	377.02

[a] *Source*: See Table II.4.

3. SOME FURTHER INTERPRETATIONS

The data in the above tables, while in considerable detail, are in a rather cubersome form for purposes of analysis. Therefore, we have prepared two summary tables which provide a more illuminating framework for interpretations. To these tables we now turn.

Using these tables, we can make a number of comparisons. From Table II.11. we can first look at intertemporal behaviour, both for the total sample and for the two sets of groupings. Because in this table we have the data for two time periods, we can carry out not only inter-group comparisons but also *intra-group* comparisons. Such intra-group comparisons are not possible in Table II.12. Second, we can carry out inter-group comparisons and comparisons with the total sample, for each of the two time periods. Such comparisons can be carried out for both sample sizes. These comparisons can help to highlight the significance of disaggregation of this study.

We concentrate on Table II.11. first. While we must be careful in making statements about causality on the basis of the data here, this table nevertheless offers some interesting information. For example, from columns (1) to (3) we see that over the period 1950–60 to 1965–73, for the forty countries, the average growth rate increased by less than one percentage point in spite of the fact that foreign capital increased rather substantially. Does it mean that foreign capital, somehow, became less productive? Or is this result merely the consequence of aggregation bias? To check this second possibility, we now turn to the two groupings as well as disaggregation of foreign capital into its component parts.

From columns (1), and (4) to (9), we can note the following. In terms of growth rate, the maximum gain was experienced by income group II, and it is this group which also experienced maximum increase in terms of total capital flows (as a % of GNP). In terms of capital inflows, in fact, they almost doubled (in ratio form) for all three groups, even though the growth performance of these groups are quite different. Thus, an unambiguous statement about the relationship between foreign capital and growth for all three groups cannot be made. However, some clue for this asymmetrical behaviour may be found if we look at the time profile of the three components of capital flows. We find that in terms of aid, group I gained most over the period – almost three times of what the ratio was in 1950–70, whereas, for group II it is foreign private investment which increased most. Could then the superior performance of group II countries be ascribed to increased foreign private investment? Is foreign private investment more productive than other forms of foreign capital inflows? We will look at evidence on these questions in the subsequent chapters.

In terms of the performance of the various geographical areas, we notice a slightly different scenario. The maximum gain in growth rate was experienced by Africa. But this region also experienced the maximum inflow of

TABLE II.11.[a]
Summary data on the sample for forty countries, 1950–60 and 1965–73

Variable[b]	Total sample		Income groups						Geographical groups					
			I		II		III		Asia		Africa		Latin America	
	1950–1960–	1965–1973–	1950–1960–	1965–1973–	1950–1960–	1965–1973–	1950–1960–	1965–1973–	1950–1960–	1965–1973–	1950–1960–	1965–1973–	1950–1960–	1965–1973–
(1)	(2)	(3)	(4)	(5)	(6)	(7)	(8)	(9)	(10)	(11)	(12)	(13)	(14)	(15)
G	5.02	5.97	4.07	4.33	4.65	6.07	5.86	6.55	6.45	7.02	3.56	4.88	4.63	5.34
S/Y	13.51	16.13	9.81	12.45	13.12	13.81	16.00	18.45	13.57	17.16	11.23	12.68	14.35	15.24
F/Y	1.99	4.41	1.28	2.78	2.39	5.41	2.11	4.13	1.34	3.36	1.26	4.39	2.72	4.67
AID	1.09	2.06	1.09	3.09	1.61	2.16	0.70	1.79	1.14	2.28	0.54	1.70	1.53	2.44
FPI	0.80	1.27	0.35	–0.58	0.53	1.61	1.28	1.57	0.52	0.29	1.63	1.34	0.70	1.42
RFI	0.10	1.09	–0.16	0.27	0.25	1.64	0.14	0.77	–0.32	0.80	–0.32	1.36	0.49	0.82

[a] *Source*: Tables II.4.–II.10.
[b] *G*: growth rate; *S/Y*: saving rate; *F/Y*: total foreign capital inflows as % of GNP; *AID*: total foreign aid as % of GNP; *FPI*: foreign private investment as % of GNP; and *RFI*: other foreign inflows as % of GNP.

TABLE II.12.[a]
Summary data on the sample for fifty-two countries, 1965–73

Variable [b]	Total sample	Income groups			Geographical groups		
		I	II	III	Asia	Africa	Latin America
(1)	(2)	(3)	(4)	(5)	(6)	(7)	(8)
G	5.91	4.44	6.19	6.73	7.03	4.92	5.27
S/Y	15.97	12.41	15.44	18.92	17.19	13.98	15.44
F/Y	3.93	3.04	4.84	3.86	3.29	4.09	4.37
AID	2.12	2.72	2.31	1.55	1.87	2.29	2.33
FPI	1.03	–0.12	1.49	1.51	0.43	1.27	1.40
RFI	0.77	0.44	1.04	0.80	0.99	0.53	0.64

a *Source*: Tables II.4.–II.10.
b See Table II.11. for notations.

foreign capital. In terms of the components of foreign capital, a rather interesting further point is that the ratio of foreign aid tripled for Africa, whereas it only doubled for the other two regions. Thus, unlike our observation in terms of income groups, we find here that countries with higher foreign aid, not foreign private investment, experience higher growth rates. The question of relative productivity of foreign aid vis-à-vis foreign private investment and other types of capital inflows remains worthy of further investigation.

In terms of Table II.12. no such inter-temporal comparisons are possible. However, we can look at the inter-group picture. First, the growth experience of various groups, compared to each other and the total sample, is somewhat different, though the statistical significance of this difference is doubtful. Second, whether income groups or geographical regions, those with the highest ratio of foreign capital inflows to their GNP do not happen to be those with the highest growth rates. What is more, in this case the correspondence between different types of foreign capital and growth which we observed before no longer holds.

So far we have said virtually nothing about the behaviour of savings rates vis-à-vis that of capital inflows. Consider Table II.11. again. For the total sample, both the ratio of savings and total capital inflows to GNP went up from 1950–60 to 1965–73. The same behaviour is exhibited by the three components of the inflows. In terms of intra-group behaviour, all three groups show patterns similar to that of the total sample over the two time periods, the only exception being *FPI* for Income Group I where it has in fact declined.

Regarding inter-group behaviour, we notice that in terms of the savings rate, maximum increase we recorded by Income Group I and Asia. However, in terms of the ratio of total capital inflow, the biggest increase took place in Income Group II and Africa.

From this belief discussion, it is difficult to suggest any definite causal relationships. However, we do note that there are substantial differences between the different income groups and between the different geographical groups. This strongly points out to the need for estimating the role of capital inflows not only at the aggregate level but also for different groupings.[4] This is indeed the approach followed in the subsequent chapters.

CHAPTER III

FOREIGN CAPITAL AND GROWTH

The role of foreign capital as a determinant of growth in the developing countries is a controversial subject. The controversy has sometimes been focussed on all foreign capital inflows and sometimes on its components, particularly foreign aid and private foreign investment. According to the orthodox position, see, for example, Rosenstein-Rodan [53] and Chenery and Strout [11], all capital inflows constitute net additions to an LDC's productive resources, thus increasing its growth rate. The channel of this effect was sometimes in the spirit of the well-known Harrod-Domar model and at other times in terms of the 'two-gap' models, where these inflows facilitated and accelerated growth by removing foreign exchange and/or domestic savings gaps. This orthodox position was challenged by radical economists like Griffin and Enos [25] and Weisskoff [66], among others. According to their line of argument foreign capital inflows exercised a depressing effect on the savings propensities of the developing countries, thus leading to a reduction of the domestic saving rates and lower rates of capital formation and consequently lower rates of growth, once again along the lines of the Harrod-Domar model. Thus unlike the orthodox position, they took the view that foreign capital, in particular, foreign aid, was a substitute and not a complement to domestic savings. These two rather extreme positions were attacked by Papanek [45] who argued that truth was somewhere in between and proposed a more pragmatic and less doctrinaire approach to the question, which essentially boils down to saying that the data should be allowed to answer the questions in a suitably formulated model.

In a detailed study Stoneman [58] suggested that private foreign investment exercises two kinds of influences on an LDC's economy; namely, the balance of payments effect which is due to the *flow* of private foreign investment and the structural effect which is due to the *stock* (defined as cumulated flows) of this investment. A priori, he suggested, the signs of these two effects cannot be determined. More recently, using a simulation model Grinols and Bhagwati [26] [1] showed that there was some justification for the position taken by the radical economists but at the same time showed that alternative outcomes were also likely under plausible assumptions and further that the adverse effects may well be reversed once dynamic considerations (say growth effects) were taken into account.

Gupta [30] pointed out that the above studies [2] made the basic mistake that they only allowed for the direct effects of foreign capital inflows on growth and did not properly specify the indirect effects through savings. Consequently, even if the qualitative position taken by the radical economists and the pragmatic approach of Papanek, Stoneman and others, is correct, they may have greatly exaggerated the quantitative magnitudes involved. This issue is considered at length in Chapters V, VI, and VII.

The aim of this chapter is to review some of the single equation studies in this area and present results of our own model. The scheme of this chapter is as follows. Section 1 critically reviews the findings of Papanek, Stoneman and Gupta. Section 2 specifies our single equation model. In Section 3 we present the results of our model at the aggregate level. The next section is devoted to the presentation of disaggregated results for the two groupings. The chapter concludes with some final remarks.

1. REVIEW OF SOME OF THE RECENT EMPIRICAL STUDIES

There have been several attempts at measuring the impact of both domestic and foreign resources on the actual growth performance of the developing countries. We confine our review to three studies: those of Papanek [48], Stoneman [58] and Gupta [33]. The main reason for selecting the first two studies is that they report the most thorough and detailed results using single equation models. Gupta's study is selected because it was the first study to use a simultaneous equations approach. However, for purposes of comparison with Papanek and Stoneman we will use the estimates of the structural equations from Gupta's model.

There are some differences in the equations estimated by Papanek and Gupta on the one hand and Stoneman on the other. The basic equation used by Papanek [3] and Gupta involved regressing growth rates on the savings rate and three components of foreign capital inflows, namely, foreign aid, private foreign investment and other foreign inflows. Stoneman, on the other hand, aggregated foreign aid and other inflows together and used cumulated private foreign investment (a stock measure) as a separate variable to capture the structural effects of private foreign investment. Thus his results are not strictly comparable with those of the other two studies. However, we still can make broad comparisons, which, as we will see, are quite revealing. All three studies use cross-section data and therefore, share the shortcomings of studies based on cross-country analysis. The sample size and the time periods covered by these studies are somewhat different. Thus Papanek combined the data for the 1950s and the 1960s with a total of 85 observations. Gupta's sample consisted of 40 countries for the 1960s while Stoneman's preferred sample consisted of 188 observations based on the data for the early 1950s, the late 1950s, the early 1960s and the late 1960s. The results are given in Table III.1.

TABLE III.1.
Regression results of some previous studies[a]

Variables \ Equation No.	1	2	3
Author	Papanek	Gupta	Stoneman[b]
Constant	1.5 (2.5)	3.57 (na)	1.088 (2.29)
(S/Y)	0.20 (6.0)	0.08 (1.4)	0.252 (9.27)
AID	0.39 (5.8)	0.16 (2.7)	0.318 (8.57)
FPI	0.17 (2.5)	0.195 (1.36)	0.076 (1.37)
RFI	0.19 (2.1)	0.298 (2.097)	
FPIC			−0.029 (3.41)
$\bar{R}^2$	0.37•	0.296	0.369
N = (sample size)	85	40	188

[a] The figures in parentheses beneath the coefficients are t-ratios.
[b] Net aid is combined with other flows, i.e. *AID also includes RFI.*

In this table, S/Y denotes the savings rate, *AID* for foreign aid, *FPI* for foreign private investment, *RFI* for other foreign inflows, *FPIC* for cumulated foreign private investment, y for per capita income and P for population.

Papanek's results (Equation 1) suggest the following:

(i) The explanatory variables explain about one-third of the cross-section differences in growth rates.

(ii) Domestic savings and different types of foreign capital inflows have positive and significant impact on growth.

(iii) Foreign aid has the largest quantitative impact on growth vis-à-vis domestic savings and other two types of inflows.

In fact, its coefficient is twice as large as the other coefficients.

Equation 2 in Table III.1. is due to Gupta [33]. The results are broadly similar, except the following:

(i) The coefficient of domestic savings is very small and appears not to be very significant.

(ii) Unlike Papanek, the coefficient of 'other' inflows has the largest coefficient and also the coefficient of *FPI* is greater than that of *AID*.

The results of Stoneman's model are shown in Equation 3 of Table III.1. We can observe the following:

(i) The coefficient of *FPI* while positive, is not statistically significant and is small in magnitude.

(ii) The coefficient of *FPIC* is negative and highly significant, thus indicating that the structural effect of foreign direct investment is to retard growth. This result thus would seem to provide empirical support for views put forward by Griffin and others against the orthodox position.

(iii) Domestic savings have a highly significant effect.

(iv) The coefficient of *AID* is also highly significant and slightly greater than the coefficient of domestic savings, thus supporting Papanek's and Gupta's findings, keeping in mind the fact that *AID* here also includes other foreign capital inflows.

A Critique of the Above Studies

The studies reviewed in Section 1 suffer from many theoretical and statistical shortcomings. Some of these shortcomings are summarized below:

(i) The explanatory variables included explain only about one-third of the cross-sectional differences in growth rates. Even for cross-section data, this must be considered fairly unsatisfactory.

(ii) The magnitude of the constant term is large and varies from 1.5 to 3.57 indicating that the countries included in the various samples will grow at a rate between 1.5 to 3.5% per annum even in the absence of any domestic savings and foreign capital inflows. This implication is clearly implausible, given the historical record about the growth performance of these economies. The large constant term, as we know, theoretically may reflect the influence of omitted variables. It is therefore plausible to assume that these studies may have excluded some important explanatory variables. One of the variables that immediately comes to mind is the contribution of labour force.

(iii) If it can be shown that some explanatory variables that do belong to the model are excluded from the set of regressors, then the coefficient estimates of these studies are generally biased unless it can be demonstrated that the omitted and the included variables are orthogonal. In general, the assumption of orthogonality is not plausible in this context.

(iv) These studies implicitly assumed that the productivity of domestic savings and different types of foreign capital inflows was the same *regardless* of the state of development in which different countries operated and managed their resources. We believe that an appropriate framework should allow these productivities to vary across countries depending on their state of development.[4]

(v) In some regressions (not reported here) Papanek used per capita income as one of the explanatory variables and its sign turned out to be negative. Surprisingly, he did not provide any theoretical justification for its inclusion nor did he offer any explanation for the observed negative sign. We shall show how per capita income can appear as one of the regressors and act as a proxy for the state of development of a country. We shall also explain how its coefficient can have either a positive or a negative sign.

(vi) Stoneman's paper defined *AID* as consisting of both foreign aid and other capital inflows. This is, however, not an appropriate procedure, because it is not difficult to speculate that factors determining the two types of inflows could be quite different.

(vii) Both Papanek and Stoneman combined cross-section data belonging to different time periods. But while Papanek performed at least simple tests to justify such pooling, no tests whatsoever were performed by Stoneman. Inappropriate pooling can lead to results which are not economically meaningful. We will have more to say about this topic later on.

(viii) It is difficult to see why Stoneman confined himself to examining the effect of cumulated foreign direct investment only rather than to all flows. It may well be that had he done so, he may have found that aid was not a significant variable either.

(ix) Stoneman's use of the lag structure for the stock variable is very curious. For example, he states that "the growth rate for the late sixties was associated with the stock as estimated at 1968, but also 1963, 1958, and 1953" (p. 16). It is difficult to see any rationale for the use of these benchmark dates. Furthermore, it is impossible to tell from his estimated equations as to which particular stock figure was in fact used. Consequently, one cannot put much reliance on his estimates of the coefficient of this variable.

(x) Stoneman does not quite explain why the flow of the variable behaves in one way and its stock in another way. This leads him into making strange policy recommendations. For example, because the effect of the flow of private foreign investment is found to be positive, he recommends encouragement of this inflow. But because the effect of the stock is negative, he proposes to "reduce the stock in order to grow faster" (p. 20). But, leaving aside the problems of measurement, how would a country reduce the stock without reducing its flow?

(xi) Stoneman reported that the stock of foreign capital did not have a significant coefficient when he estimated his model for Asia, Africa and Latin America separately. He went on to say that this "result is indeed not inconsistent with what would be expected for the case of a weak association when the sample size is reduced" (Stoneman, [58], p. 18). However a more plausible explanation may well be that his aggregative results are merely the outcome of aggregation bias and the true results are those reflected in the regional groups. That this can often happen is quite well-known.[5]

(xii) Finally, as already pointed out, Papanek's and Stoneman's studies being single equation models, suffer from the problem of simultaneity because they ignore interdependence between savings and growth.

2. THE MODEL

In this section, we develop a single equation model of growth which explicitly allows for the fact that the effect of foreign capital may depend on the stage of economic development of a country.

Before proceeding to the specification of the model, we define the variables to be used as follows: Y: Gross national product (GNP). $G = \Delta Y/Y$: Annual compound rate of change of GNP. P: Size of mid-year population. $y = Y/P$: GNP per capita. L: Active labor force. $GL = \Delta L/L$: Growth rate of labor force (annual). S/Y: Ratio of domestic savings to GNP. $AID = F_1/Y$: Ratio of foreign aid to GNP. $FPI = F_2/Y$: Ratio of foreign direct investment to GNP. $RFI = F_3/Y$: Ratio of other capital inflows to GNP. SD: A proxy for state of development. EN/L: Energy consumption per worker. K: Capital stock. I: Investment (net).

We start the specification of our model by assuming a neoclassical production function with neutral technical change:

(1) $Y = A(t) F(K, L)$.

Differentiating (1) and taking discrete approximations, we can show that

(2) $$\frac{\Delta Y}{Y} = \frac{\Delta A}{A} + MPP_K \left(\frac{\Delta K}{Y}\right) + MPP_L \frac{L}{Y} \left(\frac{\Delta L}{L}\right),$$

where MPP_K and MPP_L represent the marginal physical product of capital and labor, respectively. The term $(MPPL \cdot L)/Y$ denotes the share of labor and is assumed to remain constant, to be denoted by c. Equation (2) may then be written as

(3) $$G = \frac{\Delta Y}{Y} = \frac{\Delta A}{A} + MPP_K \left(\frac{\Delta K}{Y}\right) + c \frac{\Delta L}{L}.$$

We allow the rate of technical change $(\Delta A)/A$ and the marginal physical product of capital to vary across countries depending on the state of development (SD). For this purpose, we postulate the following relationships:

(4) $$\frac{\Delta A}{A} = \alpha_0 + \alpha_1 (SD)^{\beta_1},$$

which is a simple non-linear relationship between the rate of technical change and the state of development.

Now, for an open economy

(5) $$\Delta K = I = S + F,$$

where F stands for total foreign capital inflows. Following Papanek, we divide F into three categories:

(6) $$F = F_1 + F_2 + F_3.$$

We now assume simple but plausible non-linear relationships between various marginal productivities and the state of development as follows:

(7) $$MPP_S = \alpha_2 + \alpha_3 (SD)^{\beta_2}.$$

(8) $$MPP_{F_1} = \alpha_4 + \alpha_5 (SD)^{\beta_3}.$$

(9) $$MPP_{F_2} = \alpha_6 + \alpha_7 (SD)^{\beta_4}.$$

(10) $$MPP_{F_3} = \alpha_8 + \alpha_9 (SD)^{\beta_5}.$$

(11) $\beta_1 = \beta_2 = \beta_3 = \beta_4 = \beta_5 = 1$ for linearity.

Substituting (4)–(11) into (3) we get:

$$(12) \qquad G = [\alpha_0 + \alpha_1 (SD)] + [\alpha_2 + \alpha_3 (SD)] (\frac{S}{Y})$$
$$+ [\alpha_4 + \alpha_5 (SD)] (\frac{F_1}{Y}) + [\alpha_6 + \alpha_7 (SD)] (\frac{F_2}{Y})$$
$$+ [\alpha_8 + \alpha_9 (SD)] (\frac{F_3}{Y}) + \alpha_{10} (\frac{\Delta L}{L}) + \mu ,$$

where $A_{10} = c$ in Equation (3). Substituting *AID* for (F_1/Y), *FPI* for (F_2/Y), *RFI* for (F_3/Y) and *GL* for $(\Delta L/L)$ in Equation (12) and rearranging we get the empirical form of our model:

$$(13) \qquad G = \alpha_0 + \alpha_1 (SD) + \alpha_2 (\frac{S}{Y}) + \alpha_3 (\frac{S}{Y}) (SD) + \alpha_4 (AID)$$
$$+ \alpha_5 (AID) \cdot (SD) + \alpha_6 (FPI) + \alpha_7 (FPI) \cdot (SD)$$
$$+ \alpha_8 (RFI) + \alpha_9 (RFI) \cdot (SD) + \alpha_{10} (GL) + \mu ,$$

where μ is a random error term. The coefficients $\alpha_2, \alpha_4, \alpha_6, \alpha_8$, and α_{10} are the relevant marginal products when they are independent of the state of development and thus are expected to have positive signs. The signs of the other coefficients cannot be specified *a priori* because they depend on the behaviour of an economy at different stages of development. In general, we can expect their signs to be positive, but we cannot rule out negative signs.

3. THE EMPIRICAL RESULTS

The model was estimated using cross-section data for fifty-two developing countries.[6] The results are given in Table III.2.

As a first step, we estimated a limited version of this model so that we could carry out comparison for the 1970s with the results reported in Table III.1. for the earlier periods. The results of this limited model are given in column (1) of Table III.2. A comparison of this column with Table III.1. reveals a number of interesting things. For example:

(i) The explanatory power of the same model for the 1970s has improved somewhat.

(ii) The effect of domestic savings continues to be significant and what is more striking, the magnitude is quite close to that reported by Papanek and Stoneman for the earlier periods.

TABLE III.2.
Empirical results of the model[a]

Variables \ Equation No.	1	2	3	4	5	6
Constant	0.008 (0.94)	0.002 (0.15)	−0.002 (0.18)	−0.005 (0.05)	−0.0005 (0.05)	−0.003 (0.36)
S/Y	0.22 (4.01)	0.23 (3.58)	0.21 (4.44)	0.22 (3.49)	0.25 (6.06)	0.26 (5.94)
AID	0.30 (2.25)	0.13 (0.50)	0.31 (2.36)	0.32 (2.39)	0.13 (0.88)	0.29 (2.0)
FPI	0.17 (1.49)	0.16 (0.53)	0.16 (1.48)	0.17 (1.51)	0.13 (1.22)	0.13 (0.49)
RFI	0.35 (2.49)	0.39 (1.62)	0.37 (2.75)	0.43 (3.28)	0.37 (2.87)	0.44 (3.24)
		−0.000003 (0.14)	0.00001 (1.60)			
GL		0.032 (1.45)	0.04 (2.24)	0.04 (2.18)	0.03 (1.73)	0.04 (1.97)
(*S/Y*) (*y*)		0.00002 (0.26)		0.00002 (0.92)		
(*AID*) (*y*)		0.0004 (0.91)			0.0003 (2.0)	
(*FPI*) (*y*)		−0.00003 (0.09)				0.00004 (0.15)
(*RFI*) (*y*)		−0.00001 (0.09)				
$\bar{R}^2$	0.44	0.44	0.47	0.48	0.53	0.44

[a] Figures in parentheses are '*t*' values.

(iii) The effect of *AID* also reveals the same pattern. However, the coefficient of foreign aid does not exceed that of the savings rate to the same extent as before. Does it mean that over time, *ceteris paribus*, domestic savings have become more productive, say, due to the inflows of foreign aid?

(iv) Foreign private investment displays rather interesting behavior. On the one hand, it continues to be statistically insignificant, thus contrary to Papanek's findings but consistent with those of Gupta and Stoneman. Its magnitude is identical to that reported by Papanek for the earlier periods.

(v) The coefficient of other inflows (*RFI*) is highly significant and in fact exceeds that of all of the other variables. This result is consistent with the earlier findings of Gupta but not Papanek.

On the whole, if we confine ourselves to the simple single equation model and to the total sample, we conclude that domestic capital formation and foreign capital continue to be significant determinants of growth in developing countries.

We now turn to the estimates of the complete model which are reported in column (2) of Table III.2. Per capita income (y) is used as a proxy variable to represent the state of development.[7] It can be seen from this column that with the exception of the savings rate variable (S/Y), all other variables have statistically insignificant coefficients. This is mainly due to severe multicollinearity. For example, the simple correlation coefficient between y and S/Y is 0.52; between (S/Y) and (S/Y) (y) 0.74; between *FPI* and (*FPI*) (y) 0.87 and between *RFI* and (*RFI*) (y) 0.75. Consequently we were obliged to follow a somewhat restricted approach. Therefore we estimated the model using only one variable at a time to represent the state of development.[8] These results are reported in columns (3) to (6) of Table III.2.[9] In spite of the fact that these results are based on a limited version of the model which may lead to bias of an unknown magnitude due to the excluded variables, they nevertheless shed some interesting light on the issues under consideration. Thus we can note the following:

(i) From columns (2) and (4), we can see that the coefficient of domestic savings rate retains its significance when the related interaction variable (S/Y) (y) is also present and the coefficient of the latter is not significant. Thus, it appears that domestic savings are an important determinant of growth irrespective of the state of development.

(ii) From column (5), when the interaction term for foreign aid (*AID*) (y) enters the model, we find that the coefficient of *AID* is not significant but the coefficient of the interaction term is significant. This suggests that the aid component of foreign capital is useful only when it is associated with a higher state of development. This result is not surprising because presumably, at a higher state of development, the economy is better organized and managed and aid is more effectively utilized. On the other hand, at a lower state of development, a significant portion of aid may be used for consumption purposes rather than for capital formation. Our finding would seem to lend support to the well-known argument that in the earlier stages of development a country's capacity to absorb foreign capital for purposes of capital formation is rather limited.

(iii) From column (6) we find that private foreign investment continues to be statistically insignificant even when it enters along with its interaction term.

(iv) An additional feature of columns (5) and (6) is that the domestic savings rate continues to be significant and stable in its quantative impact.

(v) In columns (3) to (6) the growth of labor force is a significant factor even though its coefficient is quite small. This could well be due to the fact that the variable is subject to serious errors of measurement including the fact that it does not account for qualitative changes in the labor force. Labor should have been measured in efficiency units, but due to lack of appropriate data it was not possible. When we tried education as an additional variable, as a proxy for the quality of the labor force, it did not turn out to be significant.[10]

Additional support for our hypothesis that the productivities of the savings rate and the various components of foreign capital depend on the state of development can be found in Table III.3. which reports estimated productivity coefficients of the domestic savings rate (S/Y), foreign aid (AID) and private foreign investment (FPI) corresponding to three different levels of per

TABLE III.3.
Marginal productivity of domestic savings, foreign aid and foreign direct investment at different stages of development

	Typical low income country (y = US \$150)	Medium (y = \$450)	High (y = \$750)
Domestic savings (S/Y)	0.223	0.229	0.235
Foreign aid	0.175	0.265	0.355
Foreign private investment	0.136	0.148	0.160

Note: Relevant calculations in this table are derived from Table III.2.

capita income.[11] We can see from Table III.3. that the productivity of domestic savings and private foreign investment remains almost the same across the three income groups but the productivity of foreign aid increases from 0.13 for a low income country to a high of 0.35 for a high income country. These results thus support the findings of Table III.2. It is also evident from this table that for a typical low income country, marginal productivity of domestic savings is the highest followed by *AID* and *FPI*, respectively. The ranking changes for medium and high income groups, i.e., *AID* takes precedence over domestic savings and *FPI*. The performance of *FPI* is always found to be inferior than that of domestic savings or foreign aid.

4. FURTHER ANALYSIS OF GROUP ESTIMATES

In this section we report some further results on the basis of geographical and income groupings.

We have already argued how the effect of foreign capital inflows might vary across countries depending on their level of ecohnomic development. However, our efforts to estimate the complete model failed because of severe multicollinearity between the savings rate, the three components of the foeign capital inflows and the corresponding interaction terms. An alternative procedure to handle this problem is to subdivide the sample according to different levels of per capita income and identify these differing levels with different stages of economic development. This is the procedure we adopt in this section. Fifty-two countries in our sample are divided into three income groups: (i) fifteen countries in the first group (I) with $y \leqslant \$300$ (U.S.); (ii) sixteen countries in the second group (II) with $\$300 < y < \$600$; and (iii) the third group (III) with $y \geqslant \$600$ having twenty one countries.[12]

Economists like Galbraith [19] have, on the other hand argued that socio-political factors also play a significant role in determining the growth performance of a country and have suggested that such factors could be captured by classifying countries according to geographical areas. Consequently, we also estimated our model by subdividing our sample into three geographical groups, namely, Asia, Africa and Latin America.

Table III.4. gives some summary statistics of the growth rate variable for different income and geographical groups. In this table, column (1) and (2) represents mean growth rate and standard deviation of growth rate, respectively, while lowest and highest growth rate in the group is reported in columns (3) and (4), respectively. For the total sample, the mean growth rate is 5.91 with a standard deviation of 2.48. The lowest growth rate during

TABLE III.4.
Mean and standard deviation of growth rates in different groups

	Mean growth rate (%)	Standard deviation of growth rate	Lowest growth rate in the group	Highest growth rate in the group
PANEL A: INCOME GROUPS				
Total Sample	5.91	2.48	−0.9	12.7
(a) Group I (*N* = 15)	4.4	1.58	3.0	7.4
(b) Group II (*N* = 16)	6.2	2.05	2.6	10.9
(c) Group III (*N* = 21)	6.7	2.74	1.4	0.217
PANEL B: GEOGRAPHICAL REGIONS				
(a) Asia [a] (*N* = 18)	7.0	2.95		12.7
(b) Africa and Europe [b] (*N* = 13)	5.4	2.25	−0.9	8.0
(c) Latin America (*N* = 21)	5.3	1.84	1.4	9.0

[a] The high growth rate for Asia is partly attributed to the appearance of Japan, Saudi Arabia and Republic of Korea in the sample. All these three countries have a very high growth rate during the sample period 1960–73.
[b] Four European countries in this group are (i) Spain, (ii) Portugal, (iii) Greece, (iv) Malta.

this period (1965–73) was achieved by Chad (= −0.9% per annum) and highest growth rate of 12.7% was recorded by Saudi Arabia. In panel A, we find that the II and the III income groups had considerably higher growth rates (above 6%) compared to the lowest income group (only 4.4%). A similar pattern is observed for standard deviation. Of course, the difference in terms of mean and standard deviation of growth rates between group II and III is not substantial. In panel B, summary statistics for geographical groups are given in which we observe that Asia experienced a much higher rate of growth, on average, than African and Latin America. The difference in the mean growth rate between Africa and Latin America is not significant though. In terms of dispersion, Asia has the highest standard deviation followed by African and Latin America, respectively. Given the above results, the question naturally arises why certain groups of countries (such as income group II and III or countries in Asia) were experiencing much higher growth rates on the average, than countries in other groups? Are these differences in performance related to productivity differences of different types of foreign capital inflows? How far factors other than foreign capital inflows are responsible for these observed differences? We will try to explain these differences in the remaining parts of this chapter. A list of the countries in different income and geographic groups is given in Appendix A.

The regression results for the three income groups and three geographic groups are given in Table III.5. We first consider columns (1) to (3) which report the results for the three income groups. These results suggest the following:

(i) The coefficient of the domestic savings rate (S/Y) is highly significant for both the polar income groups, thus reinforcing our previous finding that this variable is significant irrespective of the state of development. Note, however, that the size of the coefficient varies considerably across the three income groups, with the highest value belonging to income group III. This result is, once again, consistent with the calculations of Table III.3.

(ii) The coefficient of foreign aid (*AID*) is significant only for the highest income group, which again supports our earlier finding that this variable is most useful at somewhat higher level of development. We have already seen that the highest income group was also experiencing the highest growth rate compared to the other two income groups. The superior growth performance of this group can, thus, be attributed to higher productivity of foreign aid in these countries. If we look into Table II.4. in Chapter II, we find that countries in this group had the lowest ratio of foreign aid to GNP. This suggests that in allocating foreign aid, productivity differences were not taken account of.

(iii) Private foreign investment does not have a significant coefficient for any of the groups, thus further supporting our aggregate results. Compared to foreign aid or domestic savings, this variable has the lowest productivity.

(iv) The coefficient of the labor force growth rate is not significant for any of the income groups.

Our results for the income groups are not comparable to any of the

TABLE III.5.
Results for the two groups

	Income groups			Geographical groups		
	I (1)	II (2)	III (3)	Asia (4)	Africa (5)	Latin America (6)
Constant	−0.001 (0.12)	−0.03 (0.88)	−0.02 (1.08)	−0.02 (1.26)	−0.04 (0.28)	0.03 (1.23)
S/Y	0.23 (2.81)	0.17 (1.23)	0.35 (2.76)	0.30 (3.59)	0.28 (4.64)	0.05 (0.29)
AID	0.41 (1.39)	0.10 (0.25)	0.99 (2.43)	0.94 (3.21)	0.25 (0.72)	0.12 (0.56)
FPI	0.51 (1.42)	−0.15 (0.40)	0.11 (0.66)	0.65 (1.49)	0.16 (0.46)	0.13 (0.91)
RFI	0.19 (0.52)	0.58 (1.92)	0.64 (2.22)	0.24 (1.04)	0.53 (1.64)	0.28 (1.15)
GL	0.007 (0.24)	0.08 (1.57)	0.02 (0.44)	0.07 (1.92)	0.008 (0.27)	0.05 (1.29)
y	0.00002 (0.40)	0.00008 (1.72)	0.0000 (0.03)	0.000006 (0.90)	0.000004 (0.43)	−0.000003 (0.17)
$\bar{R}^2$	0.50	0.30	0.43	0.72	0.83	0.001
Sample size	15	16	21	18	13	21

existing studies simply because no such estimates have been reported before. However, there is one way to check their plausibility and that is by comparing them with our own aggregate results. As we have already seen, the disaggregated results and the aggregate results are qualitatively similar, thus suggesting that our aggregate results were not just a statistical artifact. These results for the income groups also suggest that models which have excluded state of development as an explicit variable determining the effectiveness of savings rates and the various components of foreign capital inflows as determinants of growth rates in the developing countries, have introduced a serious specification error in their models, thus introducing biases of unknown magnitudes in their estimates. In this sense their results, even ignoring the biases normally inherent in single equation models, are not very reliable, particularly because the arguments for or against aid and private foreign investment seem to rest on their relative quantitative impact.

We now turn to the results for the three geographical groups. They are given in columns (4) to (6) of Table III.5. From these results we can see that the model has very high explanatory power for Asia and Africa, but not for Latin America. In terms of the relative significance of the different variables, we can note the following:

(i) The coefficient of the savings rate is highly significant for Asia and Africa, but for Latin America, it is not significantly different from zero. The closeness of the estimated coefficient for this variable for Asia and Africa is also noteworthy.

(ii) Foreign aid (*AID*) seems to exercise a significant effect only in Asia. The near unity coefficient for Asia is rather interesting. It suggests that a one percent increase in foreign aid leads to approximately 0.94% increase in the growth rate for countries in this group. It is likely that most foreign aid in this group is used for capital formation whereas in Africa and Latin America, it largely goes to meet additional consumption expenditures. An analysis of the end use of foreign aid in different groups would thus be highly desirable. This result is again consistent with our results in terms of income groups. We have already seen that on the average countries in this group experienced much higher growth rates than other groups. Again, the superior performance of Asia can be attributed to higher productivity of foreign aid in Asia. Like income group III, we again observe that foreign aid as a proportion of GNP was lowest in Asia compared to Africa and Latin America (see Table II.4. in Chapter II) indicating that in allocating aid, productivity differences were not considered.

(iii) Foreign private investment exerts an insignificant influence in all regions, a result consistent with the aggregate and the income grouping results.

(iv) The growth rate of the labor force is highly significant for Asia, but not for Africa and Latin America.

Unlike the results of the income groups, here it is possible to compare our results with some other estimates. Papanek [48] estimated models for Asia and Latin America while Stoneman [58] reported results for all three regions. Their results are given in Table III.6. Since our results are based on the data for the 1970s whereas theirs for the 1950s and the 1960s, the two sets may be used to compare the effects of the various factors for the two time periods. This comparison reveals the following (Compare results from Table III.6. with relevant results of Table III.5.):

TABLE III.6.
Results of geographical groups from Papanek and Stoneman [a]

	Asia [b]		Africa [c]		Latin America [c]	
	Papanek (1)	Stoneman (2)	Papanek (3)	Stoneman (4)	Papanek (5)	Stoneman (6)
Constant	1.5 (1.5)	0.642 (0.71)	–	2.101 (2.06)	2.5 (2.7)	1.545 (2.23)
S/Y	0.21 (4.2)	0.275 (6.81)	–	0.132 (1.72)	0.11 (2.0)	0.199 (4.78)
AID	0.46 (4.46)	0.501 (4.11)	–	0.228 (1.80)	0.29 (1.7)	0.309 (3.46)
FPI	0.35 (1.7)	1.142 (2.58)	–	0.102 (0.67)	0.19 (1.4)	0.168 (1.61)
RFI	0.13 (0.8)	–	–	–	–0.06 (–0.3)	–
FPIC	–	0.018 (0.91)	–	0.020 (0.61)	–	–0.013 (1.17)
$\bar{R}^2$	0.46	0.668	–	0.351	0.11	0.224

[a] *Source*: Papanek [48] and Stoneman [58].
[b] Stoneman's *AID* is defined to include *RFI*.
[c] Papanek does not report any results for Africa.

(i) For Asia, the rate of domestic savings was a significant factor in the 1970s just as it was in the earlier periods. For Africa the significance was much greater in the latter as was the quantitative magnitude. However, for Latin America the situation is radically different. Whereas both Papanek and Stoneman reported significant results, our result shows that the effect was not significantly different from zero.

(ii) As far as the role of foreign aid is concerned, it continues to be significant for Asia in the 1970s, just as it was in the earlier periods according to the findings of both Papanek and Stoneman. For Africa, whereas the effect was marginally significant, it is not at all significant for the 1970s. Ignoring the significance aspect, the similarity of the size of the coefficient for the two periods is striking. For Latin America, Papanek reported only marginal significance whereas Stoneman highly significant effect. For the 1970s the effect is not significantly different from zero.

(iii) Finally, about the effect of private foreign investment, there is a rather close similarity for the two time periods. For Africa and Latin America, in both periods the effect was negligible, but for Asia it changed from being highly significant (Stoneman) to totally insignificant.

The findings for the geographical groups would seem to provide some support for Galbraith's position [19] that capital is a crucial constraint in a number of Asian countries, while socio-political factors are more important for some countries in Africa and Latin America.

The results of this chapter, while subject to the same fundamental criticism as those of other studies based on single equation models, establish two points fairly strongly. First, for a proper appreciation of the role of foreign capital inflows in general and its components in particular, we must allow for the dependence of their effects on the state of development of a given country. Our procedure for capturing this effect through disaggregating countries on the basis of per capita income is a highly suggestive one and we use it in the rest of this book. And second, foreign aid is the most important form of foreign capital inflows if the main aim of these inflows is to accelerate growth in the developing countries. At the same time there are sufficient exceptions to this strong result to require caution and the need for individual country studies.

CHAPTER IV

FOREIGN CAPITAL AND SAVINGS

There has been a good deal of empirical work on the determinants of savings rates in developing countries. This can be seen from the extensive bibliographies given in the survey articles by Mikesell and Zinser [43] and Snyder [56]. The aim of this chapter is limited to a brief, but critical, review of that part of this literature which is concerned with estimating the impact of foreign capital inflows on savings rates in developing countries from cross-section data and to presenting some new estimates, using single equation models. The data used and the disaggregation adopted are the same as in the last chapter.

Our rationale for presenting results based on single equation models, once again, is the same as that in the last chapter on growth and foreign capital. Since the single equation approach to this subject still continues to be quite popular, it would be useful to see in what way, if any, the relationship between foreign capital and savings has changed from 1950–60 to 1970.

Apart from this comparability, however, we present results of a model which is more general than used before, and we use more extensive data and disaggregation than previously. Therefore, this chapter, notwithstanding the shortcomings of the single equation approach, presents a number of new results.

In the first section we present the review of what we consider to be the pertinent literature. Section 2 briefly outlines the model. In Section 3 the results for the total sample are presented. The final section discusses results for the income and the geographical grouping schemes adopted in the last chapter.

1. REVIEW OF THE SELECTED LITERATURE

The role of foreign capital inflows on savings in developing countries has attracted considerable attention. Normally one would expect that such effects would be positive and the only relevant question would be the quantitative magnitudes of these effects. However, in 1963, Trygve Haavelmo proposed an intriguing hypothesis: $I(t) = a[Y(t) + H(t)]$, where I stands for gross investment, Y for gross national product and H for capital inflows. "That is to say", Haavelmo continues, "that investment ... is a function of ... income including what they get from abroad." (Haavelmo [35].) He adds, "I think we see the possible implications. It means, for example, that domestic savings could be negative if H is large enough."

Rahman [49], interpreting this to mean that domestic savings depend not only on income but also and negatively, on foreign capital inflows, tested this hypothesis. For the purpose of testing this hypothesis, Rahman introduced a slight modification. Thus postulating that $I(t) = aY(t) + bH(t)$ and since $I(t) = S(t) + H(t)$ where $S(t)$ denotes domestic savings, we get the domestic savings function $S(t) = aY(t) + b'H(t)$ where $b' = b-1$. Hence

$$(1) \qquad \frac{S(t)}{Y(t)} = a + b'H(t).$$

Using the data for 31 less developed countries from Chenery and Strout [11] he estimated Equation (1) which is reported in column (1) in our Table IV.1. On the basis of this result he concluded that it was quite likely that foreign capital was used not only for augmenting investment but also as a substitute for domestic savings. From this he advanced the behavioristic hypothesis that the governments in developing countries may, "voluntarily relax domestic savings efforts when more foreign aid is available than otherwise" (Rahman [49], p. 317). Gupta [32] argued that this hypothesis, "sounds very much like the one about the backward sloping supply curves for farm products in the less developed countries – a hypothesis now convincingly discredited" (Gupta [32], p. 215). He tested Equation (1) using the entire sample in Chenery and Strout, which consisted of 50 countries. His results are given in column (2) of Table IV.1. It can be seen from these results that they are just the reverse of those reported by Rahman. Not only did he find that the coefficient of capital inflows was positive, but also that it was not significantly different from zero. He concluded, "from this equation it would appear that foreign capital inflows have virtually no effect on domestic savings in the less developed countries" (Gupta [32], p. 215).

The next, significant and a substantially more detailed analysis, using single equation approach, was carried out by Papanek [48], whose results are reported in columns (3)–(5) of Table IV.1. He introduced one innovation of considerable importance. Instead of treating all capital inflows as a single group implying that it consisted of homogeneous components in the sense that all of them had the same effect, he disaggregated them into three parts: foreign aid, foreign private investment, and all other inflows. Turning to his results, we find a strong confirmation of Haavelmo's hypothesis, whether

TABLE IV.1.
Impact of foreign capital inflows on domestic savings:
Review of some previous studies

Explanatory variables	Rahman [49] (1)	Gupta [32] (2)	Papanek [48] (3)	(4)	(5)
Intercept	0.1427 (NA)	0.11083 (12.6)	−6.4 (−1.4)	13.3 (−3.2)	11.4 (12.1)
(*F/Y*)	−0.2473 (−2.568)	0.0310 (0.39)	−0.73 (−6.7)	−0.64 (−7.5)	
AID					−1.00 (−7.1)
FPI					−0.65 (−3.5)
RFI					−0.38 (−1.6)
ln *y*			4.1 (5.1)	3.69 (5.7)	
ln (*POP*)			0.52 (1.3)	1.60 (4.3)	
Primary export				0.28 (7.3)	0.20 (5.4)
Other exports				1.13 (5.7)	1.50 (7.0)
$\bar{R}^2$	N.A.	0.055	0.45	0.72	0.62
No. of observations	31	50	85	85	85
Time periods	1962	1962	1950s & 1960s Pooled	1950s & 1960s Pooled	1950s & 1960s Pooled

Note (i) Figures in parentheses are *t*-values.
(ii) N.A. → not available.
(iii) Dependent variable is the savings rate.

judged by the effect of total capital inflows or by their components. Further, different components do indeed seem to have different quantitative effect. Papanek, however, went on to caution about the causality of his results (Papanek [47]). In the next and the subsequent chapters we will see that apart from the question of whether these effects represent causation in the sense of Granger (Granger [21]) we will show that the single equation approach greatly exaggerates the negative effects.

2. THE MODEL

The models used are represented by the following equations:

$$(1) \qquad \frac{S}{Y} = a_0 + b_0 G + c_0 y + d_0\, DR + e_0\, (F/Y),$$

$$(2) \qquad \frac{S}{Y} = a_1 + b_1 G + c_1 y + d_1\, DR + e_1\, AID + f_1\, FPI + g_1\, RFI,$$

$$(3) \qquad \frac{F}{y} = AID + FPI + RFI,$$

where, in addition to the variables already defined, y: per capita income, DR: dependency rate (for exact definition, see Appendix D).

A summary of the arguments for the inclusion of rate of growth of income, per capita income, and dependency rate can be found in the survey paper by Mikesell and Zinser [43]. The inclusion of the rate of growth of income has been suggested, among others, by Houthakker [37], Modigliani [45] and Swamy [60]. Growth of income as an independent explanatory variable in explaining savings behaviour is justified on the ground that a rapid increase in the rate of per capita income growth changes relative income and life-time consumption patterns, and increase transitory income in relation to permanent income, the former being more strongly and directly influencing savings rate. Therefore, given this formulation, we will expect a positive relationship ($b_0 >$ 0) between G and (S/Y). Per capita income also appears as an additional explanatory variable in the savings function. This variable is expected to have a positive effect on saving rate. The inclusion of this variable in the savings function will account for differences in the state of development of a country in a particular period of time.

The case for the inclusion of the dependency rate has been persuasively argued by Leff [41]. Dependency rate is related to birth rate and the latter has significant impact on the age distribution of the population. Following

Modigliani–Brumberg–Ando's (MBA) 'life cycle' hypothesis, it is postulated that age distribution of population will influence the savings behaviour. Leff has formulated an empirical model in which he used dependency rate (*DR*) variable to reflect the age composition of the population and in this formulation, dependency rate will exert negative influence on the savings rate, because as the percentage of dependents in the population increases, the potential for savings decreases as additional people have to be provided with the given resources.

The role of foreign capital inflows, measured as an aggregate, has been examined by Rahman [49], Gupta [32], Griffin-Enos [25], Chenery and Eckstein [10], Landau [40], Weiskoff [66], Dacy [15] among others as already pointed out in Section 1 of this chapter. Papanek has argued that it is more appropriate to treat the different components of total inflows as heterogeneous, exerting quantitatively (and even qualitatively) different effects on savings rates. In order to explicitly test the hypothesis that different components of total capital inflows exercise significantly different impact, we have specified two versions of the savings function, namely, Equations (1) and (2). Given the controversy with regard to the impact of foreign capital on savings and the existing stage of knowledge in this matter, it is not possible, on prior grounds, to sign the coefficient of the capital inflow variables. In other words, we allow the data to determine the qualitative and quantitative impact of capital inflows on savings rates in the developing countries.

3. THE RESULTS

The results of our models are given in Table IV.2. From these results we can make the following observations:

(i) From columns (1) and (2) of Table IV.1. and column (1) of this table, we can see that the results for the 1970s are more in conformity with those reported by Rahman for the 1960s rather than those by Gupta. Even more significant is the fact that the coefficient of total inflows is more than twice that in Rahman's paper.

(ii) Comparing column (5) of Table IV.1. and column (2) of Table IV.2., we find that the results for the 1970s when the total inflows are disaggregated, are sharply different from those reported by Papanek for the 1950s and the 1960s.[1] There is almost a complete reversal of the results. Whereas in Papanek, foreign aid and foreign private investment were found to be highly significant, in our case these two types of inflows do not have a statistically significant effect. What is more, unlike Papanek, the absolute magnitude of

TABLE IV.2.
Impact of foreign capital inflows on domestic savings: Empirical results

Explanatory variables	(1)	(2)	(3)	(4)
Intercept	0.1843 (16.08)	0.1833 (12.25)	0.177202 (4.289)	0.1175 (3.414)
F/Y	−0.5179 (−3.17)			
AID		−0.7221 (−1.67)	−0.6554 (−2.071)	−0.6851 (−2.129)
FPI		−0.0778 (−0.204)	−0.1717 (−0.636)	−0.1912 (−0.6809)
RFI		−0.9715 (−2.37)	−1.2281 (−4.002)	−1.3019 (−4.330)
y			0.0000232 (2.094)	0.0000267 (2.350)
DR			−0.0357 (−1.738)	−0.0158 (−0.817)
G			0.7694 (2.062)	1.2214 (4.049)
$\bar{R}^2$	0.17	0.10	0.51	0.54
No. of observations	52	52	40	52
Time period	1970	1970	1970	1970

Note: Figures in parentheses are *t*-values.

the coefficient of foreign private investment is very small. On the other hand, the role of other foreign inflows is much more significant than that reported by Papanek. As explained earlier, our results are more consistent with ***a priori*** expectations with regard to foreign direct investment and foreign aid than Papanek's.

(iii) Columns (3) and (4) of this table report results of the Equation (2). Results in column (3) are based on a sample of forty countries which corresponds to the sample used in Gupta [30]. Its use will be explained later in

Chapter VI. But at this stage it provides an indication of the sensitivity of our results to sample size. With the exception of the dependency rate and per capita income, the results are almost identical for the two samples. In particular, we should note the consistency in the sign, magnitude and the statistical significance of the coefficients of the three capital inflow variables. From these two columns we can say that the use of aggregate inflows yields misleading information about the impact of this variable on savings rates. Further, the results reported by Papanek do not appear to be very robust and plausible.

(iv) Turning to the effects of the other three variables, the almost negligible effect of per capita income, even though statistically significant, is somewhat puzzling. On the other hand, the sharp decline in the negative effect of the dependency rate is noteworthy. Even more important is the fact that the significance of this coefficient deteriorates markedly for the second sample. A reversal of a different kind is seen for the effect of the growth rate between the two samples. Thus it would appear that the sensitivity of the results to the sample size is rather uneven. Not at all as far as the effects of per capita income and the various capital inflows are concerned, but quite marked for the other two variables. Had more data been available, it would have been useful to examine this particular type of sensitivity further.

(v) The coefficient of growth remains positive and statistically significant, irrespective of the size of the sample. This coefficient, quantitatively speaking, increases from 0.77 for the forty country sample to 1.22 for the fifty-two country sample. Our result, thus, gives positive support to one major implication of the permanent income hypothesis, namely, that average saving rate is positively related to the rate of growth of income. Singh [55] also found significant relationship between these variables and in his study, the coefficient of growth was 1.4 which is close to our result.

(vi) Finally, in Table IV.2., we find that the general model (Equation (3) and (4)) explains a very high proportion of the variation of the savings rate (R^2 = 0.58) compared to the partial model (Equation (1) and (2)) in which the foreign capital inflow is the only explanatory variable(s).

4. RESULTS FOR INCOME AND GEOGRAPHICAL GROUPS

In this section, we briefly review existing studies on this topic and present our own results. Before that, we present some descriptive material on savings rates for 1970 for the various income and geographical groups. This information is given in Table IV.3. In this table, panel A reports some summary statistics

TABLE IV.3.
Mean and standard deviations of savings rate in different sample groups: 1970

	Mean savings rate (%) 1970	S.D. of savings rate in the group	Lowest savings rate in the group (%)	Highest savings rate in the group (%)
	PANEL A: INCOME GROUPS			
Total sample (n = 52)	15.97	6.52	0.07	40.6
(a) Group I (n = 15)	12.41	5.64	0.07	20.2
(b) Group II (n = 16)	15.44	4.70	8.40	28.1
(c) Group III (n = 21)	18.92	6.90	6.4	40.6
	PANEL B: GEOGRAPHICAL REGIONS			
(a) Asia [a] (n = 18)	17.19	8.53	1.60	40.6
(b) Africa & Europe [b] (n = 13)	13.98	7.05	0.70	28.1
(c) Latin America	15.44	3.75	9.6	25.4

[a] The high savings rate for Asia is partly due to the appearance of Japan and Saudi Arabia in the sample. These two countries had a very high savings rate in the year 1970.
[b] Four European Countries in this sample group are (i) Spain (ii) Portugal (iii) Greece and (iv) Malta.

for different income groups and that of geographical groups in panel B. Mean (average) and standard deviation (around mean) of savings rate is presented in columns 1 and 2, respectively, while in column 3 and 4, we depict respectively the lowest and the highest savings rate in the respective sample group. Considering the topmost row, we find that the average savings rate for 52 countries is 15.97% with a standard deviation of 6.52. The lowest savings rate varies from 0.07% to as high as 40.6% for Japan. Considering three income groups, we find, as expected , that on average, countries in the higher income groups have considerably higher savings rates (approximately 3 percentage points higher in each case, as we move from low to high income groups). Of course, this monotonicity is not found for the dispersion of savings rate (measured by standard deviation) for which we find that income group II has the smallest dispersion compared to group I and III, although the differences are not very significant.

Turning now to the geographical groups, we find that Asia has the highest savings rate (17.9%) followed by Latin America (15.44%) with the lowest savings rate being experienced by Africa. We also observe that the disperson of savings rate is very high for the countries in Asia and Africa but lowest for the countries in Latin America. Therefore, from the summary data in Table IV.3., we find considerable differences in the performance of various income and geographic groups in our sample which highlights the importance of the disaggregated approach adopted in this study.

The earliest results for income groups were reported by Gupta [32]. They are given in Table IV.4. Unlike the results reported in Tables IV.1. and IV.2., we see here that these results offer no consistent sign pattern except in terms of the statistical significance of the coefficients. For neither of the groups is

TABLE IV.4.
Impact of total foreign capital inflows on domestic savings: Results from Gupta's study on the basis of income groups

Explanatory variables	INCOME GROUPS		
	Group I	Group II	Group III
Intercept	0.10024 (8.08)	0.10916 (11.3)	0.15393 (9.7)
F/Y	0.32588 (1.11)	−0.017188 (−0.28)	0.42197 (1.29)
$\bar{R}^2$	0.348	0.077	0.377
No. of observations	N.A.	N. A.	N. A.
Time period	1962	1962	1962

Source: Gupta [32].

Notes: (i) Figures in parentheses are t-values.
(ii) N.A. not available.
(iii) Income groupings are as follows:
Group I: up to \$124
Group II: \$125–\$249
Group III: \$250–\$675

the coefficient significantly different from zero. However, the coefficient for Group II is negative. Recall that the sign of the coefficient in Table IV.1. column (2) is positive. It may well be that this sign is being produced by the aggregation bias implicit in this equation. Once again we see the importance of a disaggregated approach.

Results for geographically disaggregated groups were first reported by Ahmed [2]. They are given in Table IV.5. The consistency of the sign of the coefficient of inflows for all of his four groups is noteworthy, although we must question the advisability of the very small sample used for the Near East. Another noteworthy feature of these results is the highly significant results for all but the African groups. Once again this raises the question whether the earlier aggregate results truly reflect the behaviour of the various groups. On the other hand, the low explanatory power of the equation for the last two groups would appear to suggest a highly unsatisfactory specification.

Turning to the results for 1970, for the income groups they are given in Tables IV.6. to IV.8., while those for the geographical groups in Tables IV.9. to IV.11. For each group, we present estimates for three specifications of the savings function.

TABLE IV.5.

Impact of total foreign capital inflows on domestic savings: Results from Ahmed's study on the basis of geographical regions

Explanatory variables	GEOGRAPHICAL REGIONS			
	South Asia & Far East	Near East	Africa	Latin America
Intercept	0.15388 (N.A.)	0.17492 (N.A.)	0.09607 (N.A.)	0.16114 (N.A.)
F/Y	−1.1428 (5.15)	−0.8516 (3.62)	−0.0241 (0.372)	−0.5710 (2.17)
R^2	0.86	0.85	0.11	0.47
No. of observations	11	7	13	19
Time period	1962	1962	1962	1962

Source: Ahmed [2].

Note: (i) Figures in parentheses are *t*-values.
(ii) N.A. not available.

TABLE IV.6.
Impact of total foreign capital inflow on domestic savings: Regression results of the simple model on the basis of income groups

Explanatory variables	INCOME GROUPS		
	Group I	Group II	Group III
Intercept	0.1724 (–6.57)	0.1638 (7.82)	0.2184 (13.96)
F/*Y*	–1.150 (–2.12)	–0.1956 (–0.561)	–0.5738 (–3.22)
$\bar{R}^2$	0.26	0.20	0.35
No. of observations	15	16	21
Time period	1970	1970	1970

Note: Figures in parentheses are *t*-values.

TABLE IV.7.
Impact of different types of foreign capital inflows on domestic savings: Regression results of the simple model on the basis of income groups

Explanatory variables	INCOME GROUPS		
	Group I	Group II	Group III
Intercept	0.0951 (2.54)	0.1526 (6.90)	0.2345 (11.6)
AID	0.89 (0.76)	0.9579 (1.28)	–2.001 (–2.56)
FPI	0.807 (0.59)	–0.455 (–0.56)	–0.2341 (0.53)
RFI	1.321 (0.96)	–1.308 (–2.28)	–1.342 (–2.72)
$\bar{R}^2$	–0.06	0.34	0.32
No. of observations	15	16	21
Time period	1970	1970	1970

Note: Figures in parentheses are *t*-ratios.

First, the form of the equation estimated by Rahman, i.e., in which the only explanatory variable is the foreign capital inflows in aggregative form (*F/Y*). In the second specification, we have disaggregated aggregate capital inflows into three components, i.e., foreign aid (*AID*), foreign private investment (*FPI*), and other capital inflows (*RFI*). And finally, a specification in which we have a more general regression model of savings behaviour as depicted by Equation (2) in Section 2. In this formulation, we have introduced, in addition to foreign capital inflows in various forms, other relevant explanatory variables such as dependency rates and growth rate of income. The rationale for providing estimates of three different specifications of the savings function is as follows. Results in Tables IV.6. and IV.9. are meant to provide some comparability with the 1962 results of Rahman and Ahmed, respectively. Tables IV.7. and IV.10. are meant to see whether the same simple specification, or Haavelmo's original hypothesis, yields some additional information, once we introduce various types of capital inflows instead of capital inflows in aggregate form. Finally, Tables IV.8. and IV.11. represent results of our more general model.

Comparing Tables IV.4. and IV.6., we notice that in 1970, compared to 1962, there are both qualitative as well as quantitative differences. In terms of the qualitative differences, in 1970 the effect of total inflows is negative for all three groups whereas it was so only for group II in 1962. Quantitatively, this effect is now statistically significant for groups I and III whereas it was insignificant for all three groups in 1962. It is only for group II that the results remain virtually unchanged between the two time periods.

A comparison of Tables IV.6. and IV.7. reveals some interesting information. The explanatory power, as measured by $\bar{R}^2$, of the simple model improves substantially for groups II and III but deteriorates for group I. In group I, the coefficient of aggregate inflows is negative and significant, but the three separate coefficients are all positive and do not significantly differ from zero. In other words, for this group, various components do not exercise any effect and this explains the very low explanatory power of this equation. We then must conclude that the results in column (1) of Table IV.6. are most likely due to aggregation errors. For group II, the results of Table IV.7. are again more interesting. *AID* now turns out to exercise a positive effect though not significant while *RFI* exercises a negative and significant effect. For group III, while qualitatively the results in Table IV.7. are consistent with those of Table IV.6., quantitatively they are different in that only two of the three components have a significant effect. Foreign private investment does not have a significant effect in any income group and under any specification of the savings function.

The main conclusions that emerge from the above discussion are: (i) that since 1962, the role of foreign capital inflows as a determinant of savings rate has undergone a significant change; and (ii) that disaggregation by income groups and by types of inflows represents a clearer picture of the relationship between these two variables.

Leaving aside these results and turning to Table IV.8., we are now in a position to look in somewhat greater detail at the results of single equation

TABLE IV.8.

Impact of different types of foreign capital inflows on domestic savings: Regression results of Equation (2) on the basis of income groups

Dependent variable = savings ratio

Explanatory variables \ Income groups	INCOME GROUPS		
	Group I	Group II	Group III
Intercept	0.1679 (2.05)	0.1386 (2.15)	0.0770 (1.28)
AID	−0.3433 (−0.42)	1.4213 (2.06)	−2.4288 (−4.83)
FPI	−0.1540 (−0.15)	−0.1146 (−0.16)	0.0067 (0.02)
RFI	0.1594 (0.18)	−1.4620 (−2.66)	−1.7953 (−5.79)
y	0.0149 (1.01)	0.0101 (1.07)	0.0444 (2.49)
DR	−0.1050 (−1.91)	−0.0452 (−1.62)	0.0274 (0.83)
G	1.8231 (2.84)	0.4833 (0.87)	0.9915 (2.76)
$\bar{R}^2$	0.61	0.54	0.76
No. of observations	15	16	21
Time period	1970	1970	1970

Note: Figures in parentheses are *t*-values.

models for income groups. Once again we confine ourselves first to a discussion of the impact of various capital inflows on domestic savings.

The first thing to notice about these results is that our model explains more than twice the variation explained by the earlier equations. Even in absolute terms, the explanatory power is quite impressive. This is true for all of the three groups. Judged by this criterion our model is a considerable improvement upon earlier specifications.

About the effects of the three types of inflows, two things emerge immediately, namely, that neither in terms of the sign nor in terms of the statistical significance, there is any consistent pattern. Thus, for example, consider the role of foreign aid. It has a negative effect for groups I and III but positive for group II. On the other hand, for group I, the effect is not statistically different from zero, while it is significant for the other two. In terms of the absolute magnitude, the negative coefficient for group III is almost twice the size of the positive coefficient for group II. Foreign private investment does not have significant effect for any of the three groups so that the difference in the signs is of no practical importance. For *RFI* – other capital inflows – this peculiar pattern continues. Thus its coefficient is positive for group I but negative for the other two. It is significant for the last two groups but not for the first. In terms of intra-group behaviour, no group displays a uniform pattern in terms of either the sign or the significance of the three variables. The main conclusion to be drawn, as before, is that no generalized statements are possible either with respect to the different incomes or with respect to the effects of the three types of inflows. Put differently, a purely aggregative approach can be highly misleading.

As far as the results for the geographical groups are concerned, our results are not strictly comparable with those of Ahmed's because of differences in the definition of the groups. We therefore confine ourselves to a discussion of the results for 1970 only. From Tables IV.9. to IV.11. we can draw the following conclusions:

(i) The explanatory power of the simple Haavelmo's hypothesis improves considerably once we use three components of inflows rather than the total as the explanatory variables (see Tables IV.9. and IV.10).

(ii) From Table IV.9., only for Asia do we find a significant and negative effect of total capital inflow, while this coefficient is not significant for the other two groups.

(iii) From Table IV.10., once again there is no consistent pattern either in terms of inter-group or in terms of intra-group comparison. Thus in no group do we find all three components having the same sign or significance. Among

TABLE IV.9.
Impact of total foreign capital inflow on domestic savings: Regression results of the simple model on the basis of geographical regions

Regions	GEOGRAPHICAL REGIONS		
Explanatory variables	Asia	Africa	Latin America
Intercept	0.1993 (10.08)	0.1531 (3.88)	0.1590 (11.25)
F/Y	−0.8270 (−2.87)	−0.1849 (−0.43)	−0.0959 (−0.405)
$\bar{R}^2$	0.34	0.03	0.0085
No. of observations	18	10	21
Time period	1970	1970	1970

Note: Figures in parentheses are *t*-values.

TABLE IV.10.
Impact of different types of foreign capital inflows on domestic savings: Regression results of the simple model on the basis of geographical regions

Regions	GEOGRAPHICAL REGIONS		
Explanatory variables	Asia	Africa	Latin America
Intercept	0.2304 (8.36)	0.0673 (1.08)	0.1638 (11.3)
AID	−2.6043 (−2.49)	1.9878 (0.85)	−0.2048 (0.58)
FPI	1.042 (0.57)	2.2613 (1.18)	0.0211 (0.08)
RFI	−1.426 (−1.81)	−0.3437 (−0.17)	−0.7614 (−1.68)
$\bar{R}^2$	0.31	0.19	0.06
No. of observations	18	10	21
Time period	1970	1970	1970

Note: Figures in parentheses are *t*-values.

TABLE IV.11.
Impact of different types of foreign capital inflows of domestic savings: Regression results of Equation (2) on the basis of geographical regions

Regions / Explanatory variables	GEOGRAPHICAL REGIONS		
	Asia	Africa	Latin America
Intercept	0.2013 (2.782)	0.017 (0.321)	0.06 (1.25)
AID	−2.592 (−3.744)	−0.4415 (−0.318)	0.2865 (0.93)
FPI	−0.6104 (−0.475)	−1.0317 (−0.631)	0.0457 (0.21)
RFI	−1.358 (−2.756)	−1.7148 (−1.536)	−0.436 (−1.18)
y	0.0023 (0.129)	0.066 (0.80)	0.077 (3.80)
DR	−0.068 (−1.336)	−0.0042 (−0.119)	0.0123 (0.50)
G	1.7752 (3.216)	2.837 (4.58)	0.2889 (0.74)
$\bar{R}^2$	0.77	0.82	0.49
No. of observations	18	10	21
Time period	1970	1970	1970

Note: Figures in parentheses are *t*-values.

the three groups, *AID* is significant only for Asia. *FPI* is not significant in any one of them although the coefficient is greater than its own standard error for Africa and *RFI* has marginal significance for Asia and Latin America.

(iv) Table IV.11., which presents results of our model, once again outperforms the other ones by a substantial margin. The explanatory power for Asia and Africa, in terms of $\bar{R}^2$, is particularly impressive. There is no evident pattern here either. Thus, *AID* is significant only for Asia, *FPI* and *RFI* are marginally significant in Africa and Latin America, respectively.

(v) Comparison of Tables IV.10. and IV.11., shows that in terms of the significance of the three coefficients, there is very little difference, but the signs of some of the coefficients change.

Before concluding this chapter, we make a few comments on the role and importance of other explanatory variables in the model in explaining savings behaviour. For this purpose, we need to concentrate on Tables IV.8. and IV.11. only which gives the estimates of the general model. In terms of income groups (Table IV.8.), per capita income has positive coefficient in all three income groups but it is significant only in group III. Dependency rate has statistically significant negative effect only in income group I but it is not significant in the other two groups. The growth rate variable has expected positive sign in all income groups but it is highly significant in group I and group III. We also find that the coefficient of growth is almost twice as large in income group I compared to income group III, and almost four times larger than the coefficient in income group II.

In terms of the geographical groups, we find that (see Table IV.11.) income per capita is significant only for Latin America and that the dependency rate variable is not statistically significant in any of the three geographical groups, although for the latter variable, the coefficient has the expected negative sign for Asia and Africa. With respect to the growth rate, we observe that the coefficient is highly significant for Asia and Africa but not for Latin America. In terms of the magnitude, the coefficient is largest for Africa, followed by Asia and smallest for Latin America.

We can draw the following conclusions from the above discussion:

(i) Even within the confines of single equation models, we have succeeded in providing a more satisfactory explanation of savings behaviour in developing countries than found in the existing studies.

(ii) We have presented far more extensive results at a disaggregated level than ever before. These results use the latest available data.

(iii) We have shown the advantages of a disaggregated approach as well as the hazards of a highly aggregative approach. Disaggregation in our analysis was introduced in two major ways. First, by disaggregating the capital inflow variable into three components and second, by allowing the aggregate sample of countries to be classified into either three income groups or three geographical groups. Both forms of disaggregation provided useful information and empirical diversity of our coefficient estimates.

(iv) Since 1962, the role of foreign capital inflows as a determinant of savings rate has undergone a significant change. The negative effect is more pronounced in 1970 than in 1962.

(v) Even for the 1970 sample, when analysis is carried out in terms of income and geographic groups, we find that foreign aid has significant negative effect in income group III and Asia only. For income group II, the coefficient of foreign aid is not only positive but highly significant as well. This result is qualitatively and quantitatively different from that found in other studies such as Papanek's.

(vi) We have found that like foreign aid the sign of foreign private investment is not consistent. Although, in the majority of the cases, it retains its negative sign, the coefficient is not statistically significant in any income group or geographical group. The coefficient of other capital inflows is observed to be consistently negative and statistically highly significant in more cases compared to foreign aid and foreign private investment.

(vii) Considering the other variables in our model, the performance of per capita income and dependency rate is not very satisfactory in terms of usual statistical criteria. But the growth rate variable performed very well in the majority of the cases of income and geographical groups. The coefficient is not only positive and statistically significant as expected, but also the size of the coefficient is large.

(viii) Our results also point out to the need for examining the mechanisms through which different variables, especially different types of capital inflows, affect savings behaviour in the developing countries. This matter is not being pursued rigorously in this study.

(ix) Although our single equation model (Equation 2 in Section 2) is more general in nature compared to other studies in examining the savings behaviour, it still suffers from many limitations. One major limitation in using single equations framework is the existence of simultaneity in the relationships involved. This question is addressed in the three subsequent chapters.

CHAPTER V

FOREIGN CAPITAL, GROWTH AND SAVINGS: IMPLICATIONS OF A SIMULTANEOUS EQUATIONS APPROACH

In the previous two chapters we reviewed some of the existing literature about the effects of foreign capital inflows on growth rates and savings rates. However, all of these studies, including our own results, concentrate only on the *direct* effects of these inflows. In this chapter we show that once we allow for their *indirect* effects, two major conclusions follow. First, the single equation models exaggerate the positive effects of capital inflows on growth and the negative effect on savings rate. Second, the findings so far could even be misleading in view of the fact that in the simultaneous equations approach we cannot rule out the possibility that the *total* effect (direct plus indirect) of capital inflows on savings rates may well be positive. In order to further highlight the significance of this approach, we will also compare the direct and total effects of dependency rates on savings rate, since this variable has emerged as one of the more significant determinants and has generated considerable attention and controversy (see Leff [41] and Gupta [31, 33]).

Apart from an earlier attempt by Gupta (Gupta [33]), there is virtually no empirical study on this topic which employs this approach. However, we must point out two studies which are somewhat relevant in this connection, namely, by Bacha (Bacha [3]) and Papanek (Papanek [48]). Consequently, in the first section these two studies are reviewed and in the second section we outline our own approach.

1. REVIEW OF BACHA AND PAPANEK STUDIES

Bacha's Model

Bacha's work [1] was meant to examine, theoretically, the impact of foreign capital inflows on output growth. However, we will show that his model suffers from crucial flaw which considerably reduces the significance of his results. Our discussion of his model proceeds in two steps. First, we reproduce his model for ready reference, using his notation. Then we offer our own critique.[2]

Bacha's model is given by the following equations:

(1) $Y_T = G(K, \bar{L}) = f(K)$,

where Y_T is domestic income, $\bar{L}$ constant labor force and K capital stock.

(2) $Y_T = C + I + X - M$,

(3) $C = cY_C$,

$I = \Delta K$,

where C is consumption, I investment, X exports and M imports. Equations (2) and (3) represent the demand side.

(4) $M - X = \Delta D - R$,

where ΔD is the net inflow of foreign capital and R for the earnings of foreign capital. This equations represents the balance of payments condition.

(5) $\Delta Y_T = f_K \Delta K = f_K I$.

Assuming a linear approximation to Equation (1)

(6) $Y_C = Y_T - R$,

where Y_C is citizen's income.

(7) $I = sY_T + \Delta D - sR$,

where $s = 1 - c$ and (7) is obtained from (2)–(4) and (6).

(8) $R = rD$,

where r is the target net after tax profit tax of foreigners.

Manipulating Equations (5), (7) and (8), he gets

(9) $$\frac{\Delta Y_T}{Y_T} = f_K s + \frac{f_K D}{Y_T} [\frac{\Delta D}{D} - sr].$$

The effect of foreign capital inflows on citizens' income and national income (Y_N) is given by his Equations (11) and (12), respectively:

(11) $$\frac{\Delta Y_C}{Y_C} = f_K s + (\frac{\Delta D}{Y_C}) (f_K - r),$$

(12) $$\frac{\Delta Y_N}{Y_N} = f_K s + (\frac{\Delta D}{Y_N}) (f_K - Vr),$$

where V is the foreign firm's propensity to remit income abroad.

It is clear from the above model that Bacha examines the effect of foreign capital inflows on growth rate by allowing only the direct effect of these inflows. That is, he considers the case where the domestic resources and the foreign capital inflows are additive and thus complements. This is, however, unfortunate and strange, because as we have already seen there is considerable body of evidence which casts serious doubts on this assumption and, in fact, suggests that foreign capital inflows serve as substitutes for domestic resources. We show below that once we allow for this effect, his conclusions reproduced above, no longer remain unambiguous.

Following the findings reported in Chapter IV, we rewrite his consumption function as

$$(3a) \qquad C = cY_c + eD.$$

With this change in the specification of his consumption function, his Equation (9), which shows the effect of capital inflows on territorial income, becomes

$$(9a) \qquad \frac{\Delta Y_T}{Y_T} = f_K s + f_K \frac{D}{Y_T}\left[\frac{\Delta D}{D} - \frac{rs}{(1-e)}\right].$$

Comparing (9a) with his (9), we can see that with $e < 1$, it follows that $rs/(1-e) > rs$. Therefore, for foreign capital inflows to have a positive effect on the growth rate of territorial income, $\Delta D/D$ will have to exceed rs by a greater margin than that postulated by him. As a simple example, if we assume, as he does that $r = 0.15$ and $s = 0.20$, and, say, $e = 0.3$, then $\Delta D/D$ will have to exceed 4.3% and not 3% for foreign capital to make a positive contribution. Since the main point of his Equation (9) is to estimate orders of magnitudes for foreign capital inflows to be effective, it is clear that our modification makes a crucial difference.

His Equation (11) above which shows the effect of foreign capital inflows on citizens' income, now becomes

$$(11a) \qquad \frac{\Delta Y_C}{Y_C} = f_K s + \frac{\Delta D}{Y_c}[f_K(1-e) - r].$$

From his Equation (11), Bacha derives two conclusions: (i) if $f_K = r$, then the effect of foreign capital inflows is zero, and (ii) for the effect to be positive, a necessary and sufficient condition is that $f_K > r$. From (11a) we can see that both these conditions are altered significantly.

First, when $f_K = r$, (11a) becomes

$$\text{(11b)} \quad \frac{\Delta Y_C}{Y_C} = f_K s + \frac{\Delta D}{Y_C}(-f_K e) = f_K s - f_K e \frac{\Delta D}{Y_C}.$$

Thus, under his condition (i) when $f_K = r$, our modification leads to a negative, and not a zero, effect of foreign capital inflows. In other words, then, a necessary condition for foreign capital inflows to have a zero effect is that $f_K > r$ and not that $f_K = r$. Further, the necessary condition is no longer sufficient. Sufficiency requires that f_K exceed r by a certain amount.

His Equation (12) above, which relates foreign capital inflows to national income, now becomes

$$\text{(12a)} \quad \frac{\Delta Y_N}{Y_N} = f_K s + \frac{\Delta D}{Y_N}[f_K(1-e) - vr].$$

He concludes that if $v < 1$, then $f_K > vr$ when $f_K = r$. However, we can see that this is no longer the case in (12a). The implication of (12a) can be brought out more sharply if we write it as

$$\text{(12b)} \quad \frac{\Delta Y_N}{Y_N} = f_K s + (1-e)\frac{\Delta D}{YN}[f_K - \frac{vr}{(1-e)}].$$

It is clear from (12b) that for foreign capital to have a positive effect, assuming $v < 1$, f_K must exceed $r/(1-e)$. In other words, given e and assuming that $1 > e > 0$, the marginal productivity of capital must exceed, and not equal, the net after tax profit rate.

Papanek's Model

Papanek estimated two separate equations to examine the effects of foreign capital inflows. One equation for the growth rate and the other one for savings rate. In order to bring out the shortcomings of his approach, we reproduce his model below:

$$\text{(1)} \quad g = a_1 + b_1 y + c_1 \text{ pop} + d_1 s + \sum_{i=1}^{3} e_{1i} f_i,$$

$$\text{(2)} \quad s = a_2 + b_2 y + c_2 \text{ pop} + \sum_{i=1}^{3} e_{2i} f_i + h_i \text{ exp.},$$

where g = growth rate, y = per capita real income, pop = population, s = savings rate, f_i's = three types of foreign capital inflows defined in the previous chapters i.e., *AID*, *FPI* and *RFI* respectively, exp. = exports.

He estimated these two equations separately, treating them as single equation models. As far as Equation (1) is concerned, we can see that this is not an appropriate procedure because 's', which determines g, is not an exogenous variable. But disregarding this strictly estimation problem, the specification suffers from a more fundamental weakness. And this has to do with his second equation. By now there is plenty of literature, both theoretical and empirical, which shows that growth rate is an important determinant of savings rate. But this variable is missing from his Equation (2). This means that while we can allow for the *indirect* effect of capital inflows in his model on the growth rate via the savings rate, we cannot do the same thing for the saving rate. As a consequence, it is difficult to say to what extent his conclusions, based on *direct* effects only, will be modified once we allow for the indirect effects. This is apart from the fact that the estimates of his parameters in equation (2) will be biased due to the omission of a relevant variable. To bring out the implications of these simultaneities more clearly, we now turn to our own models.

2. IMPLICATIONS OF SIMULTANEITY [3]

In order to consdier this issue, we start with the savings function used in Chapter IV:

$$(1) \qquad \frac{S}{Y} = a_0 + b_0 y + c_0 G + d_0 DR + e_0 \left(\frac{F}{Y}\right)$$

This equation shows the *direct* effects of the dependency rate and the foreign capital inflows.

In order to allow for the *indirect* effect of the dependency rate, we proceed as follows:

Consider the following production function:

$$(2) \qquad Y = F(K, L),$$

where Y, K and L stand for GNP, capital stock and labour, respectively.

Assuming that the production function is linear and homogeneous, it may be written in per capita terms as

$$(3) \qquad Y/P = F(K/P, L/P).$$

Now L/P represents total labour force participation rate ($TLPR$). To simplify the argument, let us write down (3) in its linear form:

$$(4) \qquad y = a_1 + b_1 k + c_1 TLPR \qquad b_1 > 0 \; c_1 > 0$$

where $y = Y/P$, $k = K/P$, $TLPR = L/P$ and P = Population size.

Following demographic theory, we postulate that total labor force participation rate, among other factors, depends on dependency rate,[4] such that

$$(5) \qquad TLPR = a_2 + b_2 DR \qquad b_2 < 0$$

Substituting (5) into (4) and then (4) in (1) for y, we get, ignoring for now the term $e_0 (F/Y)$ in (1),

$$(6) \qquad \frac{S}{Y} = (a_0 + b_0 a_1 + b_0 c_1 a_2) + b_0 b_1 k + c_0 G + (b_0 C_1 b_2 - d_0) DR \, .$$

Taking into consideration the signs of b_0, c_1 and c_2, we can see that $b_0 c_1 b_2 < 0$ and therefore the coefficient of dependency rate in Equation (6) is greater than the corresponding coefficient in (1). Thus it follows that Equation (1) underestimates the effect of dependency rate to the extent that it does not allow for the adverse effect of population growth on per capita income and hence on savings rate. Our formulation thus allows for both the demand side and the supply side effects of dependency rates.

We now turn to the *total* effects of foreign capital inflows. First, we consider the case of savings rate. In Equation (1), the partial effect of (F/Y), e_0, following the findings reported in Chapter IV, is assumed to be negative.

Following Papanek we specify the following simple equation for growth:

$$(7) \qquad G = a_3 + b_3 S/Y + c_3 \left(\frac{F}{Y}\right) \qquad b_3 > 0, c_3 > 0$$

Substituting (7) in (1) we get

$$(8) \qquad \frac{S}{Y} = \frac{1}{(1 - b_3 c_0)} \left[(a_0 + c_0 a_3) + b_0 y + d_0 DR + (c_0 c_3 + e_0) \left(\frac{F}{Y}\right) \right] .$$

Now $c_0 > 0, c_3 > 0$ and $e_0 < 0$. Therefore, it follows that $(c_0 c_3 + e_0) \gtrless 0$ depending on whether $c_0 c_3 > e_0$ or $c_0 c_3 < e_0$, respectively. Hence, unlike the direct effect, it is no longer possible to predict the direction of the total effect. Even if we were to assume that $c_0 c_3 < e_0$ so that the total effect of foreign capital inflows was negative, it follows that this total effect will be smaller than the direct effect. Hence we conclude that the recent debate, and our own results in the previous chapters, may have tended to exaggerate the adverse impact of these inflows on the saving rate.

Turning now to the effect on the growth rate, substitute Equation (1) in (7), giving

$$(9) \qquad G = \frac{1}{1 - c_0 b_3} [a_3 + b_3 b_0 y + b_3 d_0 DR + (b_3 e_0 + c_3)(\frac{F}{Y})]$$

The direct effect, from Equation (7) is c_3. The total effect is $(b_3 e_0 + c_3)$. Given the signs of three parameters involved, we can see that $(b_3 e_0 + c_3) \gtrless 0$ depending on whether $c_3 > b_3 e_0$ or $c_3 < b_3 e_0$, respectively. In any event, the *total* effect on the growth rate, as long as foreign capital exercises a negative effect on the domestic saving rate, is going to be smaller than the direct effect. This points out to the need for guarding against overemphasizing the growth-inducing effects of such inflows.

CHAPTER VI

FOREIGN CAPITAL, GROWTH AND SAVINGS: A SIMULTANEOUS EQUATIONS MODEL

In Chapter V, we have explained the rationale for using a simultaneous equations approach in the determination of savings rate and growth rate. In this chapter, therefore, we attempt to specify and estimate a simultaneous equations model in which both savings and growth are treated as jointly dependent variables. In addition to simultaneity, another important feature of this model is that it allows for the interaction of the socio-economic and demographic variables. The latter aspect is increasingly recognized in the literature of development economics and demographic theory. The structure describing the complete model is given in Section 1, followed by a brief discussion of each equation in the model in Section 2. The estimates of the structural equation and their discussion are carried out in Section 3. The final section compares the results with those of the 1960s.

1. THE MODEL

The model to be estimated is given below:

(1) $$\frac{S}{Y} = a_1 + b_1 y + c_1 G + d_1 DR + e_1 AID + f_1 FPI + g_1 RFI + u_2$$
$$b_1 > 0 \quad c_1 > 0 \quad d_1 < 0 \quad e_1 \gtrless 0 \quad f_1 \gtrless 0 \quad g_1 \gtrless 0.$$

(2) $$G = a_2 + b_2 \frac{S}{Y} + c_2 AID + d_2 \dot{F}PI + e_2 RFI + f_2 GL + u_2$$
$$b_2 > 0 \quad c_2 > 0 \quad d_2 > 0 \quad e_2 > 0 \quad f_2 > 0.$$

(3) $$y = a_3 + b_3 EN + c_3 TLPR + d_3 LIT + e_3 DEN + u_3$$
$$b_3 > 0 \quad c_3 > 0 \quad d_3 > 0 \quad e_3 > 0.$$

(4) $$TLPR = a_4 + b_4 DR + u_4$$
$$b_4 < 0.$$

(5) $$DR = a_5 + b_5 BR + u_5$$
$$b_5 > 0.$$

(6) $$BR = a_6 + b_6 LIT + c_6 y + d_6 ALF + e_6 IMR + f_6 FPR + u_6$$
$$b_6 < 0 \quad c_6 < 0 \quad d_6 > 0 \quad e_6 > 0 \quad f_6 < 0.$$

(7) $FPR = a_7 + b_7 ALF + c_7 BR + u_7.$
$b_7 > 0 \quad c_7 < 0.$

(8) $IMR = a_8 + b_8 LIT + c_8 y + d_8 ALF + e_8 HB + u_8$
$b_8 < 0 \quad c_8 < 0 \quad d_8 > 0 \quad e_8 < 0$

(9) $ALF = a_9 + b_9 y + u_9.$
$b_9 < 0.$

The expected signs of the various coefficients are shown immediately below them.

List of Variables

S/Y = gross domestic saving rate.
G = growth rate of GNP
y = real per capita income.
DR = dependency rate, defined as the percentage of population between 0–14 years of age.
BR = birth rate (per 1000).
FPR = female labor force participation rate.
IMR = infant mortality rate.
AID = net transfers received by governments plus official long-term borrowing as percentage of GNP.
FPI = foreign private investment which includes private long-term borrowing plus net private direct investment as percentage of GNP.
RFI = other foreign inflows which include net private transfers, net short-term borrowing, other capital (net), and errors and omissions in the balance of payments as percentage of GNP.
F = aggregate foreign capital inflows, as percentage of GNP.
EN = per capita energy consumption (measured in kilograms per capita coal equivalents).
$TLPR$ = total labor force participation rate.
DEN = population density.
LIT = literacy rate.
ALF = percentage of labour force in agriculture.
HB = number of persons per hospital bed.
GL = rate of growth of labour force.
u_i = stochastic error term.

The structural model described above consists of nine equations, each has an independent meaning and identify a behavioural relationship in the system. Usually, a structural model may consist of (a) a set of behavioural relations, (b) a set of technological and institutional conditions and finally (c) a group of definitions and identities. The above model consists only of (a) that is, all the nine equations are structural equations. All the equations in this model are expressed in linear form both in variables and parameters. The equations contained in the model are stochastic in nature because each equation has, in the right hand side, in addition to the explanatory variables, an error term u_i, to account for omitted variables and other factors affecting the relationships. They are assumed to have certain well-defined probabilistic properties. There are nine endogenous[1] variables in the model. These are: *S/Y, G, y, TLPR, DR, BR, FPR, IMR*, and *ALF*. The variables other than these are exogenous in our model. It is to be noted here that some of the endogenous variables appear as explanatory variables in some other equations indicating the existence of simultaneity in the relationships. For example, although *G* and *DR* are endogenous variables, they appear in the right-hand side of the savings rate equation as explanatory variables. Similarly for other equations. Before proceeding further, it is to be emphasized here that the coefficients estimated from the structural equations measure only the direct effect of the relevant explanatory variable on the relevant endogenous variable, in contrast to the total effect. The latter effect is given by the reduced form coefficient which incorporates both the direct and indirect effects of an exogenous variable on the relevant endogenous variable. These are described in Chapter VII in detail.

2. A BRIEF DISCUSSION OF THE STRUCTURAL EQUATIONS

We now turn to a brief discussion of each equation in the model.

2.1. *Savings Rate Equation*

This equation has already been discussed in detail in Chapter IV. The rationale for the inclusion of per capita income, growth, dependency burden and three types of capital flows is given in that chapter. We would like to mention here that in Chapter IV, the variables *y, G*, and *DR* in the savings rate equation were treated as exogenous variables, while in the simultaneous equations model, these three are not exogenous in explaining savings rate, although they appear as explanatory variables in this equation. The logic as well as the implications of this simultaneity [in terms of biases] has been explained in Chapter V. By treating the savings rate and the growth rate as jointly dependent variables, the appearance of the growth rate as an explanatory variable in the savings equation allows for the indirect effect (in addition to direct effect of foreign capital) on savings rate given by the coefficients e_1, d_1 and g_1 in Equation (1) of foreign capital inflows on the savings rate via the growth rate. Leff [41] has examined the direct effect of dependency rate on saving rate. As Leff has shown, the direct effect operates from the demand side. By treating per capita income as endogenous in the system, as we have already shown in Chapter V, we are able to take account of the dependency rate from the supply side as well and thus allow for the indirect effect.

2.2. *Growth Rate Equation*

The nature of the growth rate equation and the variables describing it are discussed in detail in Chapter III. The only difference here is that, like the savings equation, we allow for savings and growth to be jointly determined and thus allow for the indirect effects of foreign capital inflows on the growth rate via the savings rate, the latter being explained by Equation (1). Thus, in Equations (1) and (2), we find that both savings and growth determine and in turn, is determined by each other. We also observe that capital inflow variables appear in both the equations.

2.3. *Per Capita Income Equation*

This equation can be derived as follows: Let the production function of an economy be described as GNP = $f(K, L, D, Q)$ where GNP is Gross National Product, K is physical capital, L denotes labour, D denotes natural resources including land, and Q denotes quality of labour. Assuming the production function is linear and homogeneous in K, L, and D, we get $y = GNP/P = F(K/P, L/P, D/P, Q)$ where y = per capita income and P denotes population. To estimate this equation, we used per capita energy consumption (*EN*) as a proxy for per capita fixed capital [2] (K/P), total labour force participation (*TLPR*) is used for L/P, population density (*DEN*) is used as a proxy for D/P to capture the pressure of population on non-capital resources, although this is only a rough measure as pointed out by Adelman [1] and finally the literacy rate (*LIT*) is used as a proxy for the quality of labour, Q. The per capita income equation in our model allows for the role of both capital and non-capital resources and for the quality and quantity of labour force in the economy. This equation has also direct relevance for our discussion [in Chapter V] about the indirect effect of the dependency rate on the saving rate from the supply side. Another implication of the per capita income equation is that it links the relationship between per capita income and birth rate via the relationship between total labour force participation rate and dependency rate [3] [Equation (4)]. This equation is thus consistent with Okun [46] who suggested that the level of per capita income affects the birth rate [see Equation (6)] and vice versa and that a simultaneous equation model is required to account for the reverse causation. It is this reverse causation which is being captured in our per capita income equation.

2.4. *Total Labour Force Participation Rate*

We have seen that total labour force participation rate [*TLPR*] is an explanatory variable in the per capita income equation. As already explained, to account for the effect of dependency rate and hence birth rate on per capita income, we have to specify *TLPR* as an endogenous variable.[4] We have specified, following demographic theory, a very simple linear but inverse relationship between *TLPR* and dependency rate, the latter, in turn being influenced directly and positively by birth rate (see Equation 5). It is to be noted here that Gregory *et al.* use birth rate in the *TLPR* equation whereas we have used dependency rate instead.

2.5. *Dependency Rate Equation*

This equation is straightforward and its rationale, based on demographic theory, has been ably summarized by Leff. Thus, demographic theory indicates that a prolonged high birth rate will affect a population's age composition, placing a relatively large percentage of the population in the younger age bracket.[5]

2.6. *Birth Rate Equation*

This equation embodies the hypothesis put forward by Adelman [1], Becker [4], Mincer [44], Cain [6], and Schultz [54], among others. Very briefly, the inclusion of per capita income follows from the theory of consumer choice, as for example, argued by Becker. Female labor force participation rate is included as a proxy for the "opportunity income of women and their access to the labor market".[6] The inclusion of infant mortality is justified in terms of the replacement needs of a family for children.[7] The role of education has been discussed extensively in the literature on fertility and does not need any elaboration here. As for the variable *ALF*, it has been generally argued that agricultural activity is more conducive to higher birth rates than non-agricultural activity.[8] *ALF* is used here as a proxy for this degree of the non-industrialization of a country.

In this equation, we expect literacy (*LIT*) and *FPR* to have negative influence on birth rate, while *ALF* and *IMR* to have a positive effect. But the direction and magnitude of the effect of per capita income on birth rate is uncertain, that is, it can have positive or negative effect depending on the relative strength of conflicting influences operating through per capita income. The positive relationship is suggested by Gary Becker,[9] who derives the fertility relation (as demand for children) from the microeconomic theory of utility maximization. In this framework, along with bundle of consumption goods, children appear as an argument in the utility function of the consumer. Here, so long as children are not an inferior commodity, an increase in income is expected to increase the demand for children. But this view is contested by Okun [46] who argues that the income elasticity of demand for children may well be negative because, as income increases, quality expenditure per child will increase to such an extent that parents will tend to reduce their demand for children. According to Okun, the weight of the empirical evidence presented by the National Bureau indicates, for most of the income range, that income influences fertility inversely. Becker, however, interprets this inverse relation in terms of inadequate birth control knowledge of people whose per capita income is low and therefore observed to have high birth rate. To Becker, if all families had perfect control over family size (in terms of information as well as accessibility to contraceptives), the relationship would be positive. Thus, from the above discussion, it is impossible to determine, a priori, the sign of the income coefficient in the birth rate equation.

2.7. *Female Labor Force Participation Rate Equation*

Birth rate affects the supply of female labor and is therefore included as an argument of this equation.[10] It is now well recognized that female labor force participation rate is higher in largely agrarian economies (U.N. [62]) and we therefore expect a positive relationship between this variable and the level of non-industrial development where the latter is measured by the percentage of the labor force in agriculture.

2.8. *Infant Mortality Rate Equation*

This equation is similar to the one used by Adelman. The variable, number of persons per hospital bed is used as an index of the availability of health care services. The justification for the inclusion of income and literary variables is relatively obvious.

2.9. *Share of Agricultural Labor Force Equation*

From the works of Clark [14], Chenery [8] and Kuznets [39], among others, we know by now that during the process of economic development, the relative proportions of agricultural and non-agricultural activities tend to change. More specifically, the share of the former tends to decline. Using per capita income as an indicator of the level of economic development, we posit a negative relationship between *ALF* and *y*.

3. THE ESTIMATES

The model specified in the previous section was estimated for the 1970s for a sample of fity two countries, for the three income groups and for the three geographical regions, as described in Chapter II. Estimates were obtained using both the Ordinary Least Squares (*OLS*) method and the Two Stage Least Squares (2SLS) method. However, the 2SLS estimates for the two groupings were invariably bad on the basis of usual statistical criteria. Therefore, here we report only the OLS results. But for the total sample, results using both estimators are reported. '*t*' values are given in the parentheses.

The results are presented in Tables VI.1. to VI.8. The quantitative implications of these results will be discussed in the next chapter. In this section we concern ourselves with some of the qualitative aspects only. Instead of going through each equation, we concentrate on only two of the main equations, namely, the saving rate and the growth rate, first.

Looking at Table VI.9., we notice that the saving rate equation fits the income groups and the geographical groups better than the entire sample. However, the situation is not quite the same for the growth equation. In each group, there is one case where group result is less satisfactory than for the entire sample. On the whole the saving rate equation performs better than the growth rate equation. Further, given that we are using cross-section data, the explanatory power of the two equations is quite satisfactory.

Turning now to the effect of foreign capital inflows, let us look at Table VI.10. This table shows the direction of the effect on saving rate. The effect on growth rate is positive as expected and therefore it is not displayed in a separate table. However, as pointed out earlier, there is no consensus about the sign on the savings rate. In this table we notice some interesting deviations from the widely held belief, namely, that foreign capital inflows in general have a negative effect. It should be repeated that right now we are talking about *direct* effect only. From row one of this table we can see that for the total sample, *all* types of inflows have a negative effect. However, once we

TABLE VI.1.
Nine equation simultaneous model of growth for 1970s: OLS estimates

(1) $$S/Y = \underset{(3.414)}{0.1175} + \underset{(2.35)}{0.0000267\,y} + \underset{(4.049)}{1.2214\,G} - \underset{(-0.817)}{0.0158\,DR} - \underset{(-2.129)}{0.6851\,AID} -$$
$$- \underset{(-0.69)}{0.1912\,FPI} - \underset{(-4.33)}{1.3019\,RFI} \quad (\bar{R}^2 = 0.54)$$

(2) $$G = \underset{(-0.38)}{-0.0039} + \underset{(6.109)}{0.2616\,S/Y} + \underset{(2.276)}{0.3001\,AID} + \underset{(1.4201)}{0.1604\,FPI} + \underset{(3.417)}{0.4417\,RFI} +$$
$$+ 0.0398\,GL \quad (\bar{R}^2 = 0.45)$$

(3) $$y = \underset{(-0.92)}{-33.97} + \underset{(5.53)}{0.5123\,EN} + \underset{(1.167)}{10.78\,TLPR} + \underset{(1.823)}{5.569\,LIT} -$$
$$- \underset{(-0.035)}{0.0159\,DEN} \quad (\bar{R}^2 = 0.56)$$

(4) $$TLPR = \underset{(24.4)}{0.5875} - \underset{(10.44)}{0.1669\,DR} \quad (\bar{R}^2 = 0.69)$$

(5) $$DR = \underset{(4.434)}{0.7342} + \underset{(4.535)}{0.0189\,BR} \quad (\bar{R}^2 = 0.29)$$

(6) $$BR = \underset{(6.37)}{45.84} - \underset{(-2.625)}{0.1469\,LIT} - \underset{(-1.606)}{0.0029\,y} + \underset{(1.623)}{0.1273\,ALF} + \underset{(0.429)}{0.0141\,IMR} -$$
$$- \underset{(-1.609)}{0.1623\,FPR} \quad (\bar{R}^2 = 0.60)$$

(7) $$FPR = \underset{(6.35)}{31.2} + \underset{(2.849)}{0.2356\,ALF} - \underset{(-2.643)}{0.4502\,BR} \quad (\bar{R}^2 = 0.14)$$

(8) $$IMR = \underset{(3.55)}{95.52} - \underset{(-2.907)}{0.6246\,LIT} - \underset{(-1.112)}{0.0082\,y} + \underset{(2.37)}{0.4153\,ALF} +$$
$$+ 0.0097\,HB \quad (\bar{R}^2 = 0.60)$$

(9) $$ALF = \underset{(19.9)}{63.74} - \underset{(-6.393)}{0.01999\,y} \quad (\bar{R}^2 = 0.45)$$

Note: Figures in parentheses are t-values.

TABLE VI.2.
Nine equation simultaneous model of growth for 1970s: 2SLS estimates (n = 52)

(1)
$$S/Y = \underset{(0.409)}{0.0542} + \underset{(2.33)}{0.0000513}\,y + \underset{(0.75)}{0.7907}\,G + \underset{(0.394)}{0.0307}\,\mathit{DR} - \underset{(-1.492)}{0.5872}\,\mathit{AID} - \underset{(0.551)}{0.2066}\,\mathit{FPI} - \underset{(-3.261)}{1.2148}\,\mathit{RFI} \quad (\bar{R}^2 = 0.45)$$

(2)
$$G = \underset{(0.435)}{0.0075} + \underset{(2.361)}{0.2007}\,S/Y + \underset{(1.78)}{0.2561}\,\mathit{AID} + \underset{(1.35)}{0.1558}\,\mathit{FPI} + \underset{(2.542)}{0.3819}\,\mathit{RFI} + \underset{(1.99)}{0.0388}\,\mathit{GL} \quad (\bar{R}^2 = 0.43)$$

(3)
$$y = \underset{(-0.40)}{-36.19} + \underset{(1.059)}{0.3914}\,\mathit{EN} + \underset{(0.74)}{10.1791}\,\mathit{LIT} + \underset{(0.406)}{10.17}\,\mathit{TLPR} - \underset{(-0.307)}{0.418}\,\mathit{DEN} \quad (\bar{R}^2 = 0.26)$$

(4)
$$\mathit{TLPR} = \underset{(4.637)}{0.3981} - \underset{(-0.636)}{0.0372}\,\mathit{DR} \quad (\bar{R}^2 = 0.69)$$

(5)
$$\mathit{DR} = \underset{(4.78)}{0.9363} + \underset{(2.74)}{0.01369}\,\mathit{BR} \quad (\bar{R}^2 = 0.29)$$

(6)
$$\mathit{BR} = \underset{(1.012)}{36.77} - \underset{(-0.79)}{0.0999}\,\mathit{LIT} - \underset{(-0.32)}{0.0017}\,y + \underset{(1.17)}{0.311}\,\mathit{ALF} - \underset{(-0.295)}{0.0225}\,\mathit{IMR} - 0.188\,\mathit{FPR} \quad (\bar{R}^2 = 0.57)$$

(7)
$$\mathit{FPR} = \underset{(3.49)}{27.35} - \underset{(-0.056)}{0.056}\,\mathit{ALF} + \underset{(0.057)}{0.0243}\,\mathit{BR} \quad (\bar{R}^2 = 0.04)$$

(8)
$$\mathit{IMR} = \underset{(1.27)}{92.88} - \underset{(-1.47)}{0.5241}\,\mathit{LIT} - \underset{(-0.81)}{0.0145}\,y + \underset{(0.51)}{0.45}\,\mathit{ALF} + \underset{(0.2086)}{0.0091}\,\mathit{HB} \quad (\bar{R}^2 = 0.62)$$

(9)
$$\mathit{ALF} = \underset{(17.8)}{69.65} - \underset{(-6.58)}{0.02799}\,y \quad (\bar{R}^2 = 0.45)$$

Note: Figures in parentheses are t-values.

TABLE IV.3.
Nine equation simultaneous model of growth for 1970s: OLS estimates for income group I

$$(1)\quad S/Y = \underset{(2.05)}{0.1679} + \underset{(1.01)}{0.00149}\,y + \underset{(2.84)}{1.8231}\,G - \underset{(-1.91)}{0.1050}\,DR - \underset{(-0.42)}{0.3433}\,AID -$$

$$- \underset{(-0.16)}{0.1540}\,FPI + \underset{(0.18)}{0.1594}\,RFI \quad (\bar{R}^2 = 0.72)$$

$$(2)\quad G = \underset{(0.02)}{0.0003} + \underset{(3.44)}{0.2473}\,S/Y + \underset{(1.42)}{0.3974}\,AID + \underset{(1.44)}{0.4784}\,FPI + \underset{(0.55)}{0.1851}\,RFI +$$

$$+ \underset{(9.34)}{0.0098}\,GL \quad (\bar{R}^2 = 0.65)$$

$$(3)\quad y = \underset{(0.13)}{9.438} + \underset{(5.75)}{0.8641}\,EN + \underset{(0.81)}{13.8174}\,TLPR + \underset{(0.32)}{2.17}\,LIT -$$

$$- \underset{(-1.86)}{0.504}\,DEN \quad (\bar{R}^2 = 0.77)$$

$$(4)\quad TLPR = \underset{(11.03)}{0.7586} - \underset{(-5.59)}{0.2821}\,DR \quad (\bar{R}^2 = 0.70)$$

$$(5)\quad DR = \underset{(2.82)}{1.2849} + \underset{(0.12)}{0.00126}\,BR \quad (\bar{R}^2 = 0.01)$$

$$(6)\quad BR = \underset{(2.59)}{46.54} - \underset{(1.58)}{0.1530}\,LIT - \underset{(-0.06)}{0.0014}\,y - \underset{(-0.17)}{0.0302}\,ALF + \underset{(0.49)}{0.0235}\,IMR +$$

$$+ \underset{(0.56)}{0.0960}\,FPR \quad (\bar{R}^2 = 0.43)$$

$$(7)\quad FPR = \underset{(0.55)}{12.66} + \underset{(1.67)}{0.3659}\,ALF - \underset{(-0.39)}{0.2208}\,BR \quad (\bar{R}^2 = 0.19)$$

$$(8)\quad IMR = \underset{(1.69)}{180.88} - \underset{(-1.13)}{0.67}\,LIT - \underset{(-1.08)}{0.165}\,y - \underset{(-0.27)}{0.258}\,ALF +$$

$$+ \underset{(0.69)}{0.0059}\,HB \quad (\bar{R}^2 = 0.43)$$

$$(9)\quad ALF = \underset{(0.63)}{82.35} - \underset{(1.59)}{0.0753}\,y \quad (\bar{R}^2 = 0.16)$$

Note: Figures in parentheses are t-values.

TABLE VI.4.
Nine equation simultaneous model of growth for 1970s: OLS estimates for income group II (n = 16)

$$(1)\quad S/Y = \underset{(2.15)}{0.1386} + \underset{(1.07)}{0.00101\,y} + \underset{(0.87)}{0.483\,G} - \underset{(-1.62)}{0.045\,DR} + \underset{(2.06)}{1.4213\,AID} - \underset{(-0.16)}{0.1146\,FPI} - \underset{(-2.66)}{1.462\,RFI} \quad (\bar{R}^2 = 0.69)$$

$$(2)\quad G = \underset{(0.24)}{0.0066} + \underset{(1.98)}{0.275\,S/Y} - \underset{(-0.46)}{0.179\,AID} - \underset{(-0.36)}{0.1483\,FPI} + \underset{(1.88)}{0.626\,RFI} + \underset{(1.01)}{0.0507\,GL} \quad (\bar{R}^2 = 0.16)$$

$$(3)\quad y = \underset{(2.03)}{38.58} + \underset{(0.87)}{0.1163\,EN} - \underset{(-0.022)}{10.017\,TLPR} + \underset{(1.09)}{1.758\,LIT} - \underset{(-1.32)}{0.591\,DEN} \quad (\bar{R}^2 = 0.01)$$

$$(4)\quad TLPR = \underset{(13.6)}{0.6146} - \underset{(-6.89)}{0.1782\,DR} \quad (\bar{R}^2 = 0.77)$$

$$(5)\quad DR = \underset{(1.06)}{0.6468} + \underset{(1.77)}{0.0252\,BR} \quad (\bar{R}^2 = 0.18)$$

$$(6)\quad BR = \underset{(5.58)}{52.38} - \underset{(-2.27)}{0.1436\,LIT} - \underset{(-0.52)}{0.006\,y} + \underset{(0.89)}{0.1298\,ALF} + \underset{(0.37)}{0.0187\,IMR} - \underset{(-2.06)}{0.2973\,FPR} \quad (\bar{R}^2 = 0.41)$$

$$(7)\quad FPR = \underset{(1.93)}{33.41} + \underset{(1.62)}{0.350} + ALF - \underset{(-1.59)}{0.6235\,BR} \quad (\bar{R}^2 = 0.18)$$

$$(8)\quad IMR = \underset{(0.47)}{-25.88} - \underset{(-1.31)}{0.5095\,LIT} + \underset{(1.33)}{0.095\,y} + \underset{(2.24)}{1.623\,ALF} - \underset{(-0.006)}{0.00014\,HB} \quad (\bar{R}^2 = 0.35)$$

$$(9)\quad ALF = \underset{(4.99)}{58.45} - \underset{(-0.49)}{0.0118\,y} \quad (\bar{R}^2 = 0.02)$$

Note: Figures in parentheses are t-values.

TABLE VI.5.
Nine equation simultaneous model of growth for 1970s: OLS estimates for income group III ($n = 21$)

(1)
$$S/Y = \underset{}{0.0770} + \underset{(2.49)}{0.0044\,y} + \underset{(2.76)}{0.9915\,G} + \underset{(0.83)}{0.0274\,DR} - \underset{(-4.83)}{0.2428\,AID} +$$
$$+ \underset{(0.02)}{0.067\,FPI} - \underset{(-5.79)}{0.1795\,RFI} \quad (\bar{R}^2 = 0.76)$$

(2)
$$G = \underset{(-1.16)}{-0.025} + \underset{(4.16)}{0.3507\,S/Y} + \underset{(2.91)}{0.9916\,AID} + \underset{(0.69)}{0.1091\,FPI} + \underset{(3.15)}{0.6448\,RFI} +$$
$$+ \underset{(0.47)}{0.0158\,GL} \quad (\bar{R}^2 = 0.46)$$

(3)
$$y = \underset{(0.99)}{76.68} + \underset{(2.10)}{0.3151\,EN} + \underset{(2.51)}{6.4069\,TLPR} - \underset{(-0.80)}{0.681\,LIT} +$$
$$+ \underset{(0.009)}{0.0054\,DEN} \quad (\bar{R}^2 = 0.39)$$

(4)
$$TLPR = \underset{(17.56)}{0.5422} - \underset{(-6.64)}{0.1467\,DR} \quad (\bar{R}^2 = 0.70)$$

(5)
$$DR = \underset{(3.86)}{0.5631} + \underset{(5.74)}{0.0254\,BR} \quad (\bar{R}^2 = 0.63)$$

(6)
$$BR = \underset{(0.67)}{16.88} - \underset{(-0.50)}{0.1005\,LIT} - \underset{(-0.40)}{0.0013\,y} + \underset{(1.45)}{0.2381\,ALF} + \underset{(1.61)}{0.1908\,IMR} +$$
$$+ \underset{(0.69)}{0.2494\,FPR} \quad (\bar{R}^2 = 0.55)$$

(7)
$$FPR = \underset{(7.84)}{36.9} - \underset{(-1.17)}{0.1634\,ALF} - \underset{(-1.51)}{0.2753\,BR} \quad (\bar{R}^2 = 0.32)$$

(8)
$$IMR = \underset{(5.87)}{164.5} - \underset{(-4.45)}{0.113\,LIT} - \underset{(-2.72)}{0.0133\,y} - \underset{(-1.52)}{0.5326\,ALF} +$$
$$+ \underset{(1.87)}{0.0339\,HB} \quad (\bar{R}^2 = 0.78)$$

(9)
$$ALF = \underset{(6.12)}{40.07} - \underset{(-1.59)}{0.9967\,y} \quad (\bar{R}^2 = 0.12)$$

Note: Figures in parentheses are *t*-values.

TABLE VI.6.
Nine equation simultaneous model of growth for 1970s: OLS estimates for Asia
(n = 18)

---

(1)
$$S/Y = \underset{(2.78)}{0.2013} + \underset{(0.129)}{0.0012}\, y + \underset{(3.22)}{1.775}\, G - \underset{(-1.336)}{0.068}\, DR - \underset{(-3.75)}{2.592}\, AID -$$
$$- \underset{(-0.475)}{0.6104}\, FPI - \underset{(-2.756)}{1.358}\, RFI \quad (\bar{R}^2 = 0.77)$$

(2)
$$G = \underset{(-2.032)}{-0.0357} + \underset{(6.06)}{0.3507}\, S/Y + \underset{(3.78)}{1.0338}\, AID + \underset{(1.40)}{0.6004}\, FPI + \underset{(1.89)}{0.3563}\, RFI +$$
$$+ \underset{(2.25)}{0.0731}\, GL \quad (\bar{R}^2 = 0.71)$$

(3)
$$y = \underset{(1.59)}{381.5} + \underset{(18.4)}{1.244}\, EN - \underset{(-1.26)}{8.094}\, TLPR - \underset{(-0.133)}{3.0824}\, LIT -$$
$$- \underset{(-2.26)}{1.348}\, DEN \quad (\bar{R}^2 = 0.96)$$

(4)
$$TLPR = \underset{(15.08)}{0.6406} - \underset{(-7.04)}{0.2178}\, DR \quad (\bar{R}^2 = 0.76)$$

(5)
$$DR = \underset{(2.39)}{0.5719} + \underset{(3.31)}{0.0199}\, BR \quad (\bar{R}^2 = 0.41)$$

(6)
$$BR = \underset{(3.63)}{49.07} - \underset{(-1.59)}{0.169}\, LIT - \underset{(-0.66)}{0.0015}\, y + \underset{(0.26)}{0.0363}\, ALF + \underset{(0.92)}{0.045}\, IMR -$$
$$- \underset{(-1.25)}{0.187}\, FPR \quad (\bar{R}^2 = 0.75)$$

(7)
$$FPR = \underset{(5.36)}{48.5} + \underset{(2.48)}{0.3543}\, ALF - \underset{(-3.68)}{1.0301}\, BR \quad (\bar{R}^2 = 0.45)$$

(8)
$$IMR = \underset{(2.82)}{15.37} - \underset{(-2.96)}{0.1094}\, LIT - \underset{(-1.08)}{0.0118}\, y + \underset{(0.19)}{0.1178}\, ALF +$$
$$+ \underset{(0.84)}{0.0047}\, HB \quad (\bar{R}^2 = 0.69)$$

(9)
$$ALF = \underset{(15.84)}{63.82} - \underset{(-4.78)}{0.0148}\, y \quad (\bar{R}^2 = 0.59)$$

Note: Figures in parentheses are t-values.

TABLE VI.7.
Nine equation simultaneous model of growth for 1970s: OLS estimates for Africa ($n = 10$)

$$(1)\quad S/Y = \underset{(0.32)}{0.017} + \underset{(0.80)}{0.0066}\,y + \underset{(4.58)}{2.837}\,G - \underset{(-0.119)}{0.0042}\,DR - \underset{(-0.318)}{0.4415}\,AID - \underset{(-0.631)}{0.1032}\,FPI - \underset{(-1.54)}{1.7148}\,RFI \quad (\bar{R}^2 = 0.82)$$

$$(2)\quad G = \underset{(-0.55)}{-0.006} + \underset{(5.39)}{0.304}\,S/Y + \underset{(0.41)}{0.138}\,AID + \underset{(0.116)}{0.038}\,FPI + \underset{(1.86)}{0.543}\,RFI + \underset{(0.99)}{0.0254}\,GL \quad (\bar{R}^2 = 0.88)$$

$$(3)\quad y = \underset{(-0.19)}{-25.86} + \underset{(5.55)}{1.249}\,EN + \underset{(1.07)}{2.937}\,TLPR - \underset{(-0.82)}{2.021}\,LIT - \underset{(-0.15)}{0.0298}\,DEN \quad (\bar{R}^2 = 0.96)$$

$$(4)\quad TLPR = \underset{(11.93)}{0.6776} - \underset{(-5.69)}{0.2071}\,DR \quad (\bar{R}^2 = 0.80)$$

$$(5)\quad DR = \underset{(1.43)}{0.9211} + \underset{(0.92)}{0.0134}\,BR \quad (\bar{R}^2 = 0.10)$$

$$(6)\quad BR = \underset{(3.70)}{68.5} - \underset{(2.35)}{0.4393}\,LIT - \underset{(-0.60)}{0.013}\,y - \underset{(-0.50)}{0.1026}\,ALF - \underset{(-0.90)}{0.0645}\,IMR + \underset{(0.24)}{0.1910}\,FPR \quad (\bar{R}^2 = 0.77)$$

$$(7)\quad FPR = \underset{(5.36)}{48.5} + \underset{(2.48)}{0.3534}\,ALF - \underset{(-3.68)}{1.0301}\,BR \quad (\bar{R}^2 = 0.42)$$

$$(8)\quad IMR = \underset{(1.22)}{12.308} - \underset{(-0.89)}{0.0924}\,LIT - \underset{(-0.18)}{0.0183}\,y + \underset{(0.27)}{0.2702}\,ALF + \underset{(0.01)}{0.0002}\,HB \quad (\bar{R}^2 = 0.42)$$

$$(9)\quad ALF = \underset{(14.29)}{93.37} - \underset{(-5.62)}{0.0841}\,y \quad (\bar{R}^2 = 0.80)$$

Note: Figures in parentheses are t-values.

TABLE VI.8.
Nine equation simultaneous model of growth for 1970s: OLS estimates for Latin America (n = 21)

---

(1)
$$S/Y = \underset{(1.25)}{0.06} + \underset{(3.80)}{0.0077}\,y + \underset{(0.74)}{0.289}\,G + \underset{(0.50)}{0.012}\,DR + \underset{(0.93)}{0.2865}\,AID + \underset{(0.21)}{0.0457}\,FPI - \underset{(-1.18)}{0.436}\,RFI \quad (\bar{R}^2 = 0.47)$$

(2)
$$G = \underset{(1.28)}{0.027} + \underset{(0.25)}{0.0297}\,S/Y + \underset{(0.77)}{0.1338}\,AID + \underset{(0.98)}{0.1302}\,FPI + \underset{(1.20)}{0.2796}\,RFI + \underset{(1.52)}{0.0575}\,GL \quad (\bar{R}^2 = 0.12)$$

(3)
$$y = \underset{(-0.88)}{-39.69} + \underset{(2.76)}{0.194}\,EN + \underset{(0.97)}{11.08}\,TLPR + \underset{(2.66)}{9.09}\,LIT - \underset{(-1.46)}{1.6042}\,DEN \quad (\bar{R}^2 = 0.57)$$

(4)
$$TLPR = \underset{(17.66)}{0.5499} - \underset{(-7.36)}{0.1407}\,DR \quad (\bar{R}^2 = 0.74)$$

(5)
$$DR = \underset{(2.52)}{0.699} + \underset{(3.31)}{0.0235}\,BR \quad (\bar{R}^2 = 0.37)$$

(6)
$$BR = \underset{(1.69)}{24.87} - \underset{(-0.76)}{0.063}\,LIT + \underset{(0.35)}{0.0019}\,y + \underset{(3.03)}{0.4503}\,ALF - \underset{(-0.72)}{0.0349}\,IMR + \underset{(0.01)}{0.0030}\,FPR \quad (\bar{R}^2 = 0.61)$$

(7)
$$FPR = \underset{(4.88)}{29.57} - \underset{(-1.46)}{0.1927}\,ALF + \underset{(0.14)}{0.0336}\,BR \quad (\bar{R}^2 = 0.19)$$

(8)
$$IMR = \underset{(0.59)}{32.7} + \underset{(0.06)}{0.027}\,LIT - \underset{(-0.15)}{0.0041}\,y + \underset{(1.09)}{0.8497}\,ALF - \underset{(-0.14)}{0.0059}\,HB \quad (\bar{R}^2 = 0.08)$$

(9)
$$ALF = \underset{(13.62)}{63.47} - \underset{(-5.35)}{0.0309}\,y \quad (\bar{R}^2 = 0.60)$$

Note: Figures in parentheses are t-values.

TABLE VI.9.
Explanatory power of equations (1) through (9)

Equation for	All countries	Income group			Region		
		I	II	III	Asia	Africa	Latin America
S/Y	0.58	0.75	0.69	0.82	0.84	0.92	0.60
G	0.49	0.68	0.38	0.57	0.78	0.93	0.25
y	0.59	0.78	0.20	0.48	0.97	0.97	0.63
TLPR	0.69	0.70	0.77	0.70	0.76	0.80	0.74
DR	0.29	0.01	0.18	0.63	0.41	0.10	0.37
BR	0.64	0.47	0.57	0.64	0.81	0.87	0.69
FPR	0.16	0.20	0.23	0.35	0.48	0.48	0.23
IMR	0.62	0.46	0.48	0.81	0.74	0.61	0.22
ALF	0.45	0.16	0.02	0.12	0.59	0.80	0.60

Note: In this table, only $\bar{R}^2$ values are reported, not the values of adjusted $\bar{R}^2$, as a measure of explanatory power of equations.

TABLE VI.10.
Qualitative influence of capital inflows on saving rate

Sample	*AID*	*FPI*	*RFI*
All countries	–	–	–
Income group I	–	–	+
Income group II	+	–	–
Income group III	–	+	–
Asia	–	–	–
Africa	–	–	–
Latin America	+	+	–

Note: – implies negative and + implies positive direct effect of the respective explanatory variables on the savings rate.

move to the income groups, this pattern no longer exists. Similarly this uniformity does not exist for Latin America in the geographical grouping. From this we may conclude that a strictly aggregative approach can often conceal significant regional differences and the importance of the level of economic development as a determinant of the saving rate.

These implications for aggregation, or the desirability of disaggregation, become even sharper when we look at the statistical significance of the various capital inflows on the savings and the growth rates. These results are shown in Tables VI.11. and VI.12. From these tables we can draw a number of interesting inferences. First, our results reconfirm earlier findings of Papanek and Gupta that differnt components of capital inflows have different effects even in qualitative terms and even considering direct effect only. Second, there are certain consistent patterns across the two groupings. For example, foreign private investment (*FPI*) does not exercise a significant effect. *RFI* would appear to be the most important of the three types of inflows.

We now turn to a brief analysis of other equations in the model. Refering again to Table VI.9., we find that in most of the cases, group results are better than the sample for all countries. This again indicates the superiority

TABLE VI.11.[a]
Statistical significance of capital inflows on saving rate

Sample	*AID*	*FPI*	*RFI*
All countries	s	ns	s
Income group I	ns	ns	ns
Income group II	s	ns	s
Income group III	s	ns	s
Asia	s	ns	s
Africa	ns	ns	ms
Latin America	ns	ns	ms

[a] Significance is at the 5% level.

s: significant.

ns: not significant.

ms: marginally significant implying that the coefficient is greater than its own standard error.

TABLE VI.12.[a]
Statistical significance of capital inflows on growth rate

Sample	*AID*	*FPI*	*RFI*
All countries	s	ms	s
Income group I	ms	ms	ms
Income group II	ns	ns	ms
Income group III	s	ns	s
Asia	s	ms	ms
Africa	ns	ns	ms
Latin America	ns	ns	ms

[a] See Table VI.11.

of sample disaggregation into income and geographic groups. The total labour force participation equation performed extremely well in all cases of sample classification. In this equation, dependency rate variable has always the expected negative sign and is highly significant. The dependency rate equation [Equation (5)] also performs very satisfactorily. As expected, the coefficient of the birth rate retains positive sign and is highly significant in all cases of sample classification expect income group I and African sample. The performance of agricultural labour force (*ALF*), that is, Equation (9) is also very good. In this equation, the coefficient of per capita income is always negative as expected and except for income group II, the coefficient is highly significant.

In Table VI.13., we have presented the qualitative (in terms of sign) influence of the relevant explanatory variable on the corresponding endogenous variables. The relevant endogenous variable is identified in the first column while the explanatory variables are identified in the second column along with its expected sign in the bracket. Other columns refer to the relevant sample group.

Let us consider the birth rate equation. Literacy has the expected negative sign in all cases of sample classification. Theoretically, as we have seen, the sign of per capita income is uncertain. But given our data and estimates based on them, we find that per capita income has a negative influences on birth rate in almost all cases except for Latin America. Therefore, our results, in general, do not agree with those of Becker. Agricultural labour force as

TABLE VI.13.
Qualitative influence of relevant explanatory variable on Birth Rate, Female Participation Rate and Infant Mortality Rate

Endogenous variable	Explanatory variables (expected sign)	Total Sample	Income I	Income II	Income III	Asia	Africa	Latin America
	LIT (–)	–	–	–	–	–	–	–
	y (?)	–	–	–	–	–	–	+
BR	*ALF* (+)	+	–	+	+	+	–	+
	IMR (+)	+	+	+	+	+	–	–
	FPR (–)	–	+	–	+	–	+	+
FPR	*ALF* (+)	+	+	+	–	+	+	–
	BR (–)	–	–	–	–	–	–	+
	LIT (–)	–	–	–	–	–	–	+
IMR	*y* (–)	–	–	+	–	–	–	–
	ALF (+)	+	–	+	–	+	+	+
	HB (–)	+	+	–	+	+	+	–

Note: + implies positive effect, – implies negative effect of the relevant explanatory variable on the corresponding endogenous variable. ? indicates that the sign is uncertain.

percentage of total labour force (*ALF*) has the expected positive sign, except for income group I and Africa. This result indicates that countries, in which the degree of industrialization and modernization is low, in general, experience a higher birth rate. Infant mortality rate retains its expected positive sign, except for Africa, but the sign of female participation rate is not consistent. In the latter case, female participation rate is expected to have negative influence on birth rate because the greater the participation rate of women in the labour force, the higher the opportunity cost of bearing and rearing children and thus, the lower is the birth rate expected. This expectation does not seem to be confirmed from our data. The *FPR* does not seem to be reflecting the higher opportunity cost of bearing and maintaining children in the developing countries. This result is not surprising, given the institutional set up in which families in the developing countries are organized. The existence and prevalence of extended family system may allow the participating women to work outside while the other members can take care of the babies at home, requiring no extra cost in terms of money or parents' time.

In the female participation rate equation, *ALF* has the expected positive sign except for the case of income group III and Latin America. The birth rate variable, as expected, has the negative influence on female participation rate with the exception of Latin America only. We now turn to the infant mortality rate equation. Literacy has the expected negative sign [except for Latin America] and the per capita income variable also exerts negative influence on infant mortality rate as expected. The only exception in the latter case is income group II. In this equation, the sign of *ALF* is not consistent whereas the variable hospital bed [*HB*] as a proxy for the availability of health care services performs extremely badly. In most cases, it captures the wrong sign.

In Table VI.14., we have reported summary results of the statistical significance of the relevant coefficient estimates. In the birth rate equation, the statistical significance of the coefficient, in general, is quite low, although the literacy variable performs quite well. The coefficient of the female participation rate equation is quite satisfactory. The statistical significance of the coefficient of the infant mortality rate equation is not very good. In this equation, the literacy variable performs rather fairly whereas the performance of *HB* is very unsatisfactory.

4. COMPARISON WITH THE 1960S

A specialized version of our model, consisting of Equations (1)–(3) and (5)–(8) was estimated by Gupta [33] for a sample of forty countries for the 1960s. In order to compare results with his, we estimated the same version of the model for the sample countries using the 1970s data. Gupta's results for the 1960s are given in Table VI.15. and those for the 1970s corresponding to the same model are given in Tables VI.16. and VI.17. Those in Table VI.17. are based on OLS estimator and those in Table VI.17. on the 2SLS. Since Gupta's estimates are based on 2SLS, we compare Tables VI.15. and VI.17.

Once again confining ourselves to the first two equations, we notice some very distinct differences. From Table VI.15. we see that in the saving rate equation, the first two components of capital inflows (*AID* and *FPI*) have a significant effect while *RFI* is marginally significant. However, in Table VI.17.

results are different. *FPI* is no longer significant. *AID* is only marginally significant. But *RFI* now exercises the most significant effect. Similarly, significant differences are apparent in the sizes of the three coefficients. However, the signs of the coefficients are identical in the two periods. For the growth equation, the results of the two periods are closer.

TABLE VI.14.
Statistical significance of relevant explanatory variables on Birth Rate, *FPR* and Infant Mortality Rate

Endogenous variable	Explanatory variable	Total Sample	Income I	Income II	Income III	Asia	Africa	Latin America
	LIT	s	ms	s	ns	ms	s	ns
	y	ms	ns	ns	ns	ns	ns	ns
BR	*ALF*	ms	ns	ns	ms	ns	ns	s
	IMR	ns	ns	ns	ms	ns	ns	ns
	FPR	ms	ns	s	ns	ns	ns	ns
FPR	*ALF*	s	ms	ms	ns	s	s	ms
	BR	s	ns	ms	ms	s	s	ns
	LIT	s	ns	ms	s	s	ns	ns
IMR	*y*	ns	ns	ns	s	ns	ns	ns
	ALF	s	ns	s	ms	ns	ns	ns
	HB	ns	ns	ns	ms	ns	ns	ns

Note: s: implies significant as 5% level.
ns: not significant.
ms: marginal significance implying that the coefficient is marginally greater than its own standard error.

TABLE VI.15.
Seven equation model of growth for 1960s: 2SLS estimates[a]

(1) $S/Y = 9.9883 + \underset{(2.409)}{0.01516\,y} + \underset{(1.488)}{2.56851\,G} - \underset{(0.733)}{0.25293\,DR} - \underset{(2.904)}{0.78160\,AID} -$

$- \underset{(2.359)}{1.47807\,FPI} - \underset{(1.577)}{1.05435\,RFI} \quad (\bar{R}^2 = 0.241)$

(2) $G = 3.5708 + \underset{(1.415)}{0.08398\,S/Y} + \underset{(2.671)}{0.15553\,AID} + \underset{(1.362)}{0.19531\,FPI} +$

$+ \underset{(2.097)}{0.29788\,RFI} \quad (\bar{R}^2 = 0.296)$

(3) $y = 601.1077 - \underset{(1.838)}{12.6186\,DR} + \underset{(7.805)}{0.20789\,EN} - \underset{(0.690)}{0.07932\,DEN} +$

$+ \underset{(1.366)}{1.87395\,LIT} \quad (\bar{R}^2 = 0.808)$

(4) $DR = 19.9642 + \underset{(6.991)}{0.5493\,BR} \quad (\bar{R}^2 = 0.721)$

(5) $BR = 15.8009 - \underset{(1.233)}{0.53450\,FPR} + \underset{(0.326)}{0.005\,y} + \underset{(0.400)}{0.08277\,IMR} + \underset{(0.648)}{0.0762\,LIT} +$

$+ \underset{(1.030)}{0.38507\,ALF} \quad (\bar{R}^2 = 0.340)$

(6) $FPR = 33.6277 - \underset{(1.222)}{0.81558\,BR} + \underset{(1.186)}{0.30764\,ALF} \quad (\bar{R}^2 = 0.201)$

(7) $IMR = 55.2487 - \underset{(0.0416)}{0.00245\,y} + \underset{(1.234)}{0.90261\,ALF} - \underset{(1.032)}{0.39630\,LIT} -$

$- \underset{(0.098)}{0.000003\,HB} \quad (\bar{R}^2 = 0.327)$

[a] From Gupta [33].

TABLE VI.16.
Seven equation simultaneous model of growth for 1970's: OLS estimates (n = 40)

$$
\begin{aligned}
(1)\ S/Y &= \underset{(4.289)}{0.177202} + \underset{(2.094)}{0.000023\,y} + \underset{(2.062)}{0.7694\,G} - \underset{(-1.738)}{0.0357\,DR} - \underset{(-2.071)}{0.6554\,AID} - \\
&\quad - \underset{(-0.636)}{0.1717\,FPI} - \underset{(-4.002)}{1.2281\,RFI} \quad (\bar{R}^2 = 0.51)
\end{aligned}
$$

$$
\begin{aligned}
(2)\ G &= \underset{(1.431)}{0.0164} + \underset{(3.581)}{0.1963\,S/Y} + \underset{(1.62)}{0.2267\,AID} + \underset{(1.287)}{0.1479\,FPI} + \\
&\quad + 0.4625\,RFI \quad (\bar{R}^2 = 0.32)
\end{aligned}
$$

$$
\begin{aligned}
(3)\ y &= \underset{(1.742)}{794.466} - \underset{(-2.425)}{5.6104\,DR} + \underset{(4.115)}{0.4163\,EN} - \underset{(-0.519)}{0.2525\,DEN} + \\
&\quad + \underset{(1.822)}{7.3878\,LIT} \quad (\bar{R}^2 = 0.60)
\end{aligned}
$$

$$
(4)\ DR = \underset{(0.819)}{0.6437} + \underset{(4.946)}{0.0225\,BR} \quad (\bar{R}^2 = 0.39)
$$

$$
\begin{aligned}
(5)\ BR &= \underset{(4.352)}{39.45} - \underset{(-1.043)}{0.1405\,FPR} - \underset{(-1.288)}{0.0029\,y} + \underset{(0.285)}{0.0127\,IMR} - \underset{(-1.59)}{0.1159\,LIT} + \\
&\quad + \underset{(1.88)}{0.2048\,ALF} \quad (\bar{R}^2 = 0.57)
\end{aligned}
$$

$$
(6)\ FPR = \underset{(6.025)}{30.39} - \underset{(-1.978)}{0.3804\,BR} + \underset{(1.809)}{0.1961\,ALF} \quad (\bar{R}^2 = 0.08)
$$

$$
\begin{aligned}
(7)\ IMR &= \underset{(2.688)}{83.19} - \underset{(-0.72)}{0.0057\,y} + \underset{(1.49)}{0.5746\,ALF} - 0.6063\,LIT + \\
&\quad + \underset{(0.89)}{0.0098\,HB} \quad (\bar{R}^2 = 0.54)
\end{aligned}
$$

Note: Figures in parentheses are t-values.

TABLE VI.17.
Seven equation simultaneous model of growth for 1970s: 2SLS estimates (n = 40)

(1) $$S/Y = \underset{(1.129)}{0.1978} + \underset{(1.18)}{0.0000213\,y} + \underset{(0.937)}{1.1541\,G} - \underset{(-0.849)}{0.0639\,DR} - \underset{(-1.925)}{0.6678\,AID} - \underset{(-0.455)}{0.1654\,FPI} - \underset{(-2.737)}{1.3452\,RFI} \quad (\bar{R}^2 = 0.50)$$

(2) $$G = \underset{(0.629)}{0.0117} + \underset{(2.35)}{0.2213\,S/Y} + \underset{(1.613)}{0.2464\,AID} + \underset{(1.375)}{0.153\,FPI} + \underset{(3.21)}{0.4843\,RFI} \quad (\bar{R}^2 = 0.31)$$

(3) $$y = \underset{(-0.438)}{-579.77} + \underset{(0.346)}{2.70024\,DR} + \underset{(3.53)}{0.5104\,EN} + \underset{(0.264)}{0.1815\,DEN} + \underset{(1.70)}{8.139\,LIT} \quad (\bar{R}^2 = 0.49)$$

(4) $$DR = \underset{(4.046)}{0.8554} + \underset{(2.863)}{0.0165\,BR} \quad (\bar{R}^2 = 0.39)$$

(5) $$BR = \underset{(3.025)}{40.75} - \underset{(-0.405)}{0.1227\,FPR} - \underset{(-0.757)}{0.0032\,y} + \underset{(0.0044)}{0.0004\,IMR} - \underset{(-1.496)}{0.1236\,LIT} + 0.2046\,ALF \quad (\bar{R}^2 = 0.57)$$

(6) $$FPR = \underset{(4.43)}{33.002} - \underset{(-1.464)}{0.525\,BR} + \underset{(1.56)}{0.2537\,ALF} \quad (\bar{R}^2 = 0.08)$$

(7) $$IMR = \underset{(2.67)}{99.117} - \underset{(-1.075)}{0.0161\,y} + \underset{(0.754)}{0.3578\,ALF} - \underset{(-2.089)}{0.555\,LIT} + \underset{(0.624)}{0.0073\,HB} \quad (\bar{R}^2 = 0.51)$$

Note: Figures in parentheses are t-values.

CHAPTER VII

THE MULTIPLIER ANALYSIS

As pointed out in the introduction, the main objective of this study is to examine the quantitative impact of foreign capital inflows and its components on savings and growth rates using a simultaneous equations model approach. Having estimated such a model in the last chapter, we now turn to an examination of the quantitative question. For this purpose we must solve the estimated structural model so that we can estimate not only direct but also the total effects, that is, direct and indirect, of these inflows. In order to accomplish this task we will proceed as follows. In Section 1, to facilitate the reader, we provide a brief discussion of the reduced forms and the impact multipliers. Then using this methodology, in Section 2 we will compare the direct and the total effects and examine their implications. Section 3 will look at the relative importance of various exogenous variables, other than capital inflows, on saving and growth rates, by using the concept of elasticity multipliers discussed in Section 1. In the next section, we look at the role of physical capital accumulation and investment in human capital for their implications for employment, more particularly their effect on the labour force participation rates, for population growth as reflected in their effects on birth rates, and for structural transformation of an economy as reflected by the share of labour force engaged in the agriculture sector. While these questions are not the primary focus of this study, it is nevertheless useful to look at them, if only to highlight the broader implications of the approach adopted in this study. The final section is devoted to a comparison of the 1960s with the 1970s insofar as the role of capital inflows is concerned.

1. REDUCED FORMS AND THE ELASTICITY MULTIPLIERS

The coefficients of the structural equations presented in the last chapters provide what are called the *direct* effect of a given exogenous variable on the endogenous variable. For example, the coefficient of foreign aid (*AID*) in the saving rate equation in Table VI.1. is –0.6851. This represents the direct effect. As already explained in Chapter V, this does not allow for the indirect effects. In order to take account for this, the simultaneous equations models must be solved. As is well known, we do this as follows.

The system of estimated structural equations, in matrix form, can be written as

(1) $$Z = \hat{A}Y + \hat{B}X + \hat{C} = 0,$$

where

$$\hat{A} = \frac{\partial Z}{\partial Y} = \begin{bmatrix} 1 & \frac{\partial Y_1}{\partial Y_2} & \cdots & \frac{\partial Y_1}{\partial Y_m} \\ \frac{\partial Y_2}{\partial Y_1} & 1 & \cdots & \frac{\partial Y_2}{\partial Y_m} \\ \vdots & & \ddots & \vdots \\ \frac{\partial Y_m}{\partial Y_1} & \frac{\partial Y_m}{\partial Y_2} & \cdots & 1 \end{bmatrix} = \begin{bmatrix} \alpha_{11} & \alpha_{12} & \cdots & \alpha_{1m} \\ \alpha_{21} & \alpha_{22} & \cdots & \alpha_{2m} \\ \vdots & & \ddots & \vdots \\ \alpha_{m1} & \alpha_{m2} & \cdots & \alpha_{mm} \end{bmatrix}$$

$$\hat{\beta} = \frac{Z}{X} = \begin{bmatrix} \frac{\partial Y_1}{\partial X_1} & \frac{\partial Y_1}{\partial X_2} & \cdots & \frac{\partial Y_1}{\partial Z_k} \\ \frac{\partial Y_2}{\partial X_1} & & & \frac{\partial Y_2}{\partial X_k} \\ \vdots & & & \vdots \\ \frac{\partial Y_m}{\partial X_1} & \frac{\partial Y_m}{\partial X_2} & \cdots & \frac{\partial Y_m}{\partial X_k} \end{bmatrix} = \begin{bmatrix} \beta_{11} & \beta_{12} & \cdots & \beta_{1k} \\ \beta_{21} & \beta_{22} & & \beta_{mk} \\ \vdots & & & \vdots \\ \beta_{m1} & \beta_{m2} & \cdots & \beta_{mk} \end{bmatrix}$$

$$\hat{C} = \begin{bmatrix} \hat{C}_1 \\ \hat{C}_2 \\ \vdots \\ \hat{C}_m \end{bmatrix}, \quad Y = \begin{bmatrix} Y_1 \\ Y_2 \\ \vdots \\ Y_m \end{bmatrix}, \quad X = \begin{bmatrix} X_1 \\ X_2 \\ \vdots \\ X_k \end{bmatrix}$$

The unknown in equation system (1) is the $m \times 1$ vector of endogenous variables. X is the $k \times 1$ vector of predetermined variables. Solving the system for Y we get

(2) $$Y = -\hat{A}^{-1}\hat{B}X - \hat{A}^{-1}\hat{C}.$$

The product $\hat{A}^{-1}B$ is a matrix of order $m \times k$. Ignoring constant terms, (2) may be rewritten as

$$Y = \hat{\pi}X,$$

where $\hat{\pi} = -\hat{A}^{-1}\hat{\beta}$. The system (3) constitutes a set of reduced form equations because each of the endogenous variables has been expressed as a function of the predetermined variables. The coefficients of these equations are called reduced form coefficients. It is clear that every element of $\hat{\pi}$ depends on all of the coefficients of $\hat{A}$. That is why we say that the reduced form coefficients measure both the direct and the indirect effect of a given predetermined variable, with all other such variables being kept constant, on a given endogenous variable. These coefficients are sometimes called *impact* multipliers.[1]

Using this methodology, we derived reduced forms (for both OLS and 2SLS)[2] for the entire sample and for the two groupings. They are presented in Tables C1–7 in Appendix C. In these tables, the endogenous variables are given in the first column and the exogenous variables in the top row. Each cell measures the *total*, that is the direct *and* the indirect, effect of a given exogenous variable on a particular endogenous variable, keeping all other exogenous variables constant. For example, in Table C1, the second entry in the first row, –0.4681, measures the total effect of *AID* on the saving rate.

These reduced form coefficients (impact multipliers) can be used for comparing the effect of different exogenous variables on a given endogenous variable provided the exogenous variables are measured in identical units. However, if this is not so, then such comparisons are not possible. To handle this problem, we calculate 'elasticity multipliers' at the means of the variables. As is well known, this particular measure is independent of the units of measurement employed. These multipliers are presented in Tables C.8–14 of Appendix C. The order of presentation of these tables is the same as that for the reduced forms.[3]

2. DIRECT VERSUS TOTAL EFFECTS OF CAPITAL INFLOWS

In this section, we examine the *direct* and *total* effects of various types of foreign capital inflows on the saving and the growth rates. These effects are summarized in Tables VII.1. and VII.2. for the saving rate and the growth rate, respectively.

Turning first to Table VII.1., we can draw a number of conclusions:

(i) For the total sample, from the first row, we notice two things which are

TABLE VII.1.
Direct and total effect of capital inflows on saving rate [a]

Sample	Direct effect			Total effect		
	AID	*FPI*	*RFI*	*AID*	*FPI*	*RFI*
Total Sample	−0.6851	−0.1912	−1.3019	−0.4681	0.0069	−1.1204
Income Groups						
I	−0.3433	−0.1540	0.1594	0.6942	1.3078	0.9408
II	1.4213	−0.1146	−1.4620	1.5390	−0.2148	−1.3368
III	−0.2428	0.0067	−0.1795	−2.2163	0.1761	−1.7722
Regional Groups						
Asia	−2.5920	−0.6104	−1.3580	−2.0051	1.2066	−0.1299
Africa	−0.4415	−0.1032	−1.7148	−0.3606	−6.6967	−1.2605
Latin America	0.2865	0.0457	−0.4360	0.3280	0.0840	−0.3583

[a] *Source*: Tables VI.1–VI.7 and C1–C7 of Appendix C.

TABLE VII.2.
Direct and total effect of capital inflows on growth rate [a]

Sample	Direct effect			Total effect		
	AID	*FPI*	*RFI*	*AID*	*FPI*	*RFI*
Total Sample	0.3001	0.1604	0.4417	0.1776	0.1622	0.1486
Income Groups						
I	0.3974	0.4784	0.1851	0.5691	0.8018	0.4089
II	−0.1790	−0.1483	0.6260	0.2435	−0.2073	0.2590
III	0.9916	0.1091	0.6448	0.2144	0.1709	0.0233
Regional Groups						
Asia	1.0338	0.6004	0.3563	0.3306	1.0236	−0.0581
Africa	0.1380	0.0380	0.5430	0.0285	−1.9968	0.1601
Latin America	0.1338	0.1302	0.2796	0.1435	0.1327	0.2690

[a] *Source*: See Table VII.1.

in accordance with our theoretical discussion in Section V.2, where we argued that the sign of the *total* effect could be different from the *direct* effect even if direct effect was assumed to be negative. This is precisely what we find for *FPI*. The direct effect is negative but the total effect is positive. We further argued that the *total* effect may well be smaller than the direct effect. We find this to be the case for all three types of inflows. It is thus clear that the single equation models used in the literature greatly exaggerate and, even distort, the impact of foreign capital inflows on saving rates in developing countries.

(ii) Turning to the three groups, the results are even more revealing. For group I, the direct effect of *AID* and *FPI* is negative while that of *RFI* is positive. This latter effect is opposite of that observed for the total sample. In terms of the total effect, the differences are even more striking. First, all three kinds of inflows have a positive effect. Second, these effects are substantially greater than the direct effects. The results relating to group I thus show that if we were to draw our conclusions either from the total sample or from the direct effects of group I model, we would reach completely erroneous conclusions!

For group II, we again notice considerable variations between its results and those for the total sample. Thus, for the total sample and the effect of *AID* (direct as well as total) is negative while for group II it is positive. On the other hand, while the total effect for *FPI* for the total sample is positive, it is negative for group II. Comparing the direct and the total effects for the group II itself, we notice that the direct effects underestimate all of the effects. The total effects are greater than the corresponding direct effects. This result is different from that of the total sample.

For group III, we notice differences between its results and those for the total sample. We also notice inter-group differences but no intragroup differences insofar as the signs of the direct and the total effects are concerned. For the total sample, *FPI* has a negative effect while in this case the effect is positive. As far as the quantitative magnitudes are concerned, all of the total effects exceed their corresponding direct effects.

(iii) We now examine the results for the three geographical regions. First we notice that there are considerable differences between these results and those for the total sample, both qualitatively and quantitatively. For example, for Latin America, the direct effect of *AID* and *FPI* is positive while it is negative for the total sample. There are more marked differences in terms of the total effects. Thus for Africa, *FPI* has a negative effect but for the total sample, it is positive.

Turning to the intra-group differences between the two effects first, we find that for Asia the direct effect of *FPI* is negative but the total effect is positive and almost twice in size of the direct effect.

In terms of the inter-group comparison, there are some striking differences. For Asia and Africa, *AID* has a negative effect but has a positive impact in Latin America. In terms of the total effect, *FPI* has a positive effect in Asia and Latin America but negative in Africa.

Our theoretical discussion in Section V.2. is once again supported even in terms of the quantitive magnitudes. For example, for Asia the negative impacts are grossly exaggerated when we compare the total effects with the corresponding direct effects. Similarly, for Africa, except for *FPI*, direct effects overestimate the negative impact. On the other hand, the damaging effect of *FPI* is greatly underestimated if we look only at the direct effect. In Latin America, the total effects for *AID* and *FPI* exceed their direct effects while the negative effect of *RFI* is lower.

The direct and the total effects of various inflows on the growth rate are summarized in Table VII.2. In this case the major differences are in terms of the quantitative magnitudes. Consider the total sample. The total effect is smaller than the direct effect for *AID* and *RFI* and almost equal for *FPI*. This is what we should expect given the results in Row 1 of Table VII.1. and our discussion in Section V.2. with negative impact of inflows on saving rate and since saving rate is a determinant of the growth rate, the indirect negative effect via the saving rate on the growth rate reduces the positive direct effect of the various inflows on the growth rate.

In terms of the results for the three income groups, we notice some substantial differences. The most curious one is the negative direct effect of *AID* and *FPI* for group II. It is difficult to explain why this is so. On the other hand the negative total effect for *FPI* is not so difficult once we allow for the negative indirect affect from Table VII.1. Quantitatively, we notice that for group I, every total effect exceeds its corresponding direct effect. For group II, the story is the same except for the effect of *RFI* where its total effect is about half of the direct effect. Notice also the change in the sign – from negative to the positive – for *AID*. These results make sense once we allow for the indirect effects via the saving function and take note of the statistical results for group II in Table VII.1. For group III, the direct effects of *AID* and *RFI* exceed the total effects while it is reverse for *FPI*. Once again it is consistent with the results in Table VII.1.

As far as the three geographical groups are concerned, we again notice considerable inter- and intra-group differences. Thus for Asia, the total effect paints a different picture than the direct effects. *RFI* has a negative effect by the total effect criterion while positive in terms of the direct effect. Quantitatively, *AID* is more important than *FPI* if we look at the direct effect but their roles are reversed if we look at the total effects.

In case of Africa, first notice the change in sign for *FPI* as we move from direct to the total effect. Quantitatively in this case the ranking of the three types of inflows remains the same whether we look at the direct or the total effects.

For Latin America, the total effect of *AID* and *FPI* is greater than their direct effect while it is the other way round for *RFI*. However, the relative importance of the three types of inflows remains unchanged as we move from the direct to their total effects.

From the above discussion, we can draw a number of conclusions. First, as was discussed in Chapter V, a simultaneous equation model approach is better for discussing the controversy relating to the role of foreign capital inflows. As demonstrated there, we find that consideration of direct effects alone can lead to both misleading conclusions and/or under or overestimates of the quantitative impact. Further our results support the importance of disaggregation, already demonstrated in the earlier chapters. We have found very substantial differences, both qualitative and quantitative, between the results of the total sample and those for the three income groups and the three geographical regions. These differences are significant enough to suggest that as far as possible, simultaneous equations model approach at the disaggregated level is a preferred approach. Of course, the level and the type of disaggregation will be dictated by the objectives of the study being contemplated.

3. IMPORTANCE OF CAPITAL INFLOWS RELATIVE TO THAT OF OTHER FACTORS

So far we have concentrated on the effects of capital inflows only on saving and growth rates. However, given the continuing controversy about the relative importance of various factors as sources of growth, it is perhaps instructive to examine the impact of other exogenous factors. For this purpose we use the elasticity multipliers of Tables VII.3. and VII.4. Table VII.3. relates to the saving rate while Table VII.4. deals with the growth rate.

For the saving rate we notice that for the total sample, literacy rate has the highest multiplier. For the income and the regional groups, there are considerable discrepancies. Thus for group I, capital accumulation (*EN*) has

TABLE VII.3.
Elasticity multipliers for saving rate for 1970s[a]

Exogenous Variables	Total (52 Countries)	Sample					
		Income groups			Regional groups		
		I	II	III	Asia	Africa	Latin America
AID	−0.0598	0.0887	0.1965	−0.2830	0.2561	−0.0561	0.0419
FPI	0.0005	0.1030	−0.0169	0.0139	0.0950	−0.5273	0.0066
RFI	−0.0757	0.0611	−0.0903	−0.1198	−0.1299	−0.0852	−0.0242
EN	0.1163	1.2583	0.0767	0.1182	0.0888	3.1934	0.0799
DEN	−0.0004	−0.0829	−0.0440	0.0002	−0.0108	−0.0086	−0.0746
LIT	0.1387	0.0426	0.1907	−0.1257	0.3993	−0.2767	0.2961
GL	0.1108	0.0459	0.0399	0.0339	0.4853	0.7380	0.0237
HB	−0.0003	0.0001	0.00	−0.0121	−0.0030	0.00	0.00

[a] *Source*: Tables C8–C14 Appendix C.

TABLE VII.4.
Elasticity multipliers for growth rate for 1970s[a]

Exogenous variables	Total (52 Countries)	Sample					
		Income groups			Regional groups		
		I	II	III	Asia	Africa	Latin America
AID	−0.0598	0.1967	0.0842	0.0741	0.1143	0.0099	0.0496
FPI	0.0005	0.1709	−0.0442	0.0364	0.2181	−0.4255	0.0283
RFI	−0.0757	0.0748	0.0474	0.0043	−0.0581	0.0293	0.0492
EN	0.1163	0.8422	0.0570	0.1121	0.0843	2.6265	0.0064
DEN	−0.0004	−0.0555	−0.0327	0.0002	−0.0103	−0.0071	−0.0060
LIT	0.1387	0.0285	0.1418	−0.1193	0.3790	−0.2276	0.0238
GL	0.1108	0.0682	0.2234	0.0925	0.7399	0.7040	0.2216
HB	−0.0003	−0.0001	0.00	−0.0115	−0.0028	0.00	0.00

[a] *Source*: See Table VII.3.

the largest effect; for group II, foreign aid closely followed by literacy and for group III, it is again capital accumulation. In terms of the regional grouping, for Asia, growth of labour force and literacy have the highest effect; for Africa, capital accumulation, followed by literacy, and for Latin America, the leading multiplier is with respect to literacy.

The most revealing aspect of these results is that except for income group II, in no other case do any of the components of capital inflows have the dominating effect. This would seem to suggest that the role of foreign capital inflows in influencing the saving rate has been exaggerated. At the same time, the relatively better performance of foreign aid vis-à-vis foreign private investment and other foreign investment is once again noteworthy.

Turning now to Table VII.4., for the growth rate, the largest multiplier effects are as follows. For the total sample, it is literacy; for income group I, it is capital accumulation (*EN*) followed by foreign aid; for income group II, growth rate of labour force (*GL*), followed by literacy and foreign aid; for income group III, the largest effect is exerted by capital accumulation followed by foreign aid; for Asia, the ranking of the multipliers is with respect to growth rate of labour force, literacy, foreign private investment and foreign aid; for Africa, the most significant variable is capital accumulation and then the growth rate of labour force, and finally, for Latin America, the dominant variable is growth rate of labour force followed by foreign aid.

These findings for the growth rate are broadly consistent with those for the saving rate. From them two observations seem pertinent: first, that there is no getting away from the fact that domestic efforts in the form of increased literacy rates, and so on, are more important than external factors such as capital inflows; and second, that foreign aid rather than any other forms of capital inflows is the most effective form of capital inflow. Thus we have some evidence here which supports the position of those who consider foreign aid rather than foreign private investment as the more productive form of capital inflow.

4. SOME OTHER IMPLICATIONS OF THE ELASTICITY MULTIPLIERS

In this section we examine the effects of capital accumulation (*EN*) and investment in human capital (*LIT*) on three other endogenous variables of the model, namely, total labour force participation rate, the birth rate (*BR*) and the share of agricultural labour force (*ALF*). The reason for selecting these three variables for investigation is that they represent some of the most important variables that we are generally concerned with in explaining the process of economic development. Thus, total labour force participation rate affects the supply side of the employment problem; the birth rate, *ceteris paribus*, reflects the population problem and the share of the agricultural labour force is a good proxy for reflecting structural changes in an economy.

The results are given in Table VII.5. We can draw a number of interesting inferences from this table.

TABLE VII.5.
Elasticity multipliers for *TLPR*, *BR* and *ALF* with respect to *EN* and *LIT* for 1970[a]

Sample	*TLPR*		*BR*		*ALF*	
	EN	*LIT*	*EN*	*LIT*	*EN*	*LIT*
Total	(1)	(2)	(3)	(4)	(5)	(6)
	0.0217	0.1185	−0.0663	−0.3630	−0.2023	−0.1906
Income Groups						
I	0.0039	0.0116	−0.1051	−0.3155	−1.2622	−0.0260
II	0.0081	0.1747	−0.0173	−0.3759	−0.0265	−0.0302
III	0.0136	0.2146	−0.0352	−0.5565	−0.0455	−0.0020
Regional Groups						
Asia	0.0276	0.2276	−0.0614	−0.5075	−0.3559	0.0283
Africa	0.0327	0.2097	−0.1140	−0.7301	−2.0435	0.2200
Latin America	0.0182	0.1105	−0.0531	−0.3228	−0.1212	−0.4609

[a] *Source*: See Table VII.3.

(1) Total labour force participation is positively affected for the total sample as well as for the two groupings by both capital accumulation and the literacy rate, with the latter being quantitatively many times more important. This suggests that as the literacy rate rises, we can expect the total supply of labour to increase as a result of rising labour force participation rate, thus adding to the unemployment problem – a rather common phenomenon in developing countries. Our findings discussed above about the role of investment in human capital (as proxied by the literacy rate here) in accelerating growth rates, and the present finding, highlights the dilemma faced by many of the developing countries. On the one hand, investment in human capital is

required to train manpower required for accelerated growth, but at the same time it excerbates the already serious unemployment problem.

(2) Birth rate and, *ceteris paribus*, population growth rate, is negatively effected by both factors. However, here again the effects of the literacy rate are dominant for the total sample as well as for the two sets of groupings. There are considerable disparities in the quantitative magnitudes, however. These findings support what is by now well established, namely, that education does lead to lower birth rates and consequently, lower population growth rates. But notice again the nature of the dilemma involved.

(3) As far as structural changes in the developing countries are concerned, we notice that the relative significance of education and accumulation in physical capital is just the opposite to that for the birth rate for the total sample and the two groups. We might say that high rates of capital accumulation is a necessary condition for the structural transformation of the developing countries, a finding consistent with the predictions of well-known economic development models.

5. COMPARISON OF THE 1960S WITH THE 1970S

Earlier Gupta [33] published a study using a model consisting of seven simultaneous equations for forty countries for the 1960s. In order to compare the relative importance of the various types of capital inflows and other exogenous variables on the saving and growth rates for the two periods, we estimated the same model for the same sample of countries for the 1970s. The results were presented in Chapter VI. The reduced form equations for the two periods are given in Tables C15 and C16 of Appendix C and the elasticity multipliers in Tables C17 and C18 of the same Appendix.

Instead of going through a detailed comparison of the various tables for the two periods, once again we concentrate on the *direct* and the *total* effects of the various capital inflows on the saving rate and the growth rate for the two periods.

The results for the saving rate are summarized in Table VII.6. Qualitatively, the major difference is that *FPI*, in terms of the total effect, has a positive effect in 1970s as against a negative one for the 1960s. In terms of the quantitative impact, for the 1960s we find that, in terms of the total effect, the relative importance of the three types of inflows has the ranking *RFI, AID* and *FPI*. However, for the 1970s this ranking is *FPI, AID* and *RFI*. Thus *AID* continues to be in the middle. The absolute magnitude of the total effect of *AID* is also noteworthy. For the two periods, it has remained virtually the

TABLE VII.6.
Comparison with 1960s of direct and total effect of foregn capital inflows on saving rate (n = 40)

	1960s		1970s	
	Direct effect	Total effect	Direct effect	Total effect
AID	−0.7816	−0.4872	−0.6678	−0.5149
FPI	−1.4780	−1.2455	−0.1654	0.0150
RFI	−1.0543	−0.3688	−1.3452	−1.0560

[a] *Source*: Tables VI.12–13. and Table C15 and C16 of Appendix C.

same. On the other hand, the effect of *FPI* in the 1970s, though positive, is almost negligible. However, the negative effect of *RFI* in the 1970s is almost three times that of what it was in the 1960s. If we compare only the direct effects for the two periods, we would reach strikingly different conclusions!

The effect on growth rate for the two periods are given in Table VII.7. First looking at the total effects for the two periods, we notice that *RFI* was the most important type of inflow in both periods. However, the importance of the other two is reversed. In the 1960s *AID* had a greater effect than *FPI* on growth rate but their roles got reversed in the 1970s. In terms of the magnitudes, the total effect of *AID* and *RFI* in the two periods has remained

TABLE VII.7.
Comparison with 1960s of direct and total effect of capital inflows on growth rate (n = 40) [a]

	1960s		1970s	
	Direct effect	Total effect	Direct effect	Total effect
AID	0.2464	0.1146	0.2464	0.1324
FPI	0.1530	0.0905	0.1530	0.1563
RFI	0.4843	0.2669	0.4843	0.2506

[a] *Source*: See Table VII.6.

almost the same whereas that of *FPI* has gone up from 0.0905 to 0.1563. The direct effects, on the other hand, have remained almost constant between the two periods! In each time period, except in *FPI* in the 1970s, the total effect is smaller than the corresponding direct effect. This, as explained earlier, is due to the negative impact of the inflows on the saving rates.

From this discussion we may conclude that in so far as the role of the various capital inflows is concerned, there have been both qualitative and quantitative changes in their impact on saving rate and the growth rate between the 1960s and the 1970s. However, the differences are far more marked for the saving rate than for the growth rate. Our discussion also confirms the importance of treating the saving rate and the growth rate as jointly dependent variables and of disaggregating foreign capital inflows into its various components. An interesting question, not pursued here, is to figure out why the various types of inflows exercise different impacts and why does their relative influence change over time. This will be important for both policy purposes and for working out the most effective types of foreign capital assistance.

Turning to Table VII.8. which compares the total effect of all of the exogenous variables on the saving and the growth rates for the two time periods, we can notice some important changes.

(1) For the saving rate, in the 1960s the most dominant factors were the structural variables as represented by the share of the agricultural labour force

TABLE VII.8.
Elasticity multipliers for saving and growth rates for 1960s and 1970s (n = 40)[a]

Exogenous variables	Saving rate		Growth rate	
	1960s	1970s	1960s	1970s
AID	−0.1080	−0.0658	0.0657	0.0458
FPI	−0.1289	0.0012	0.0242	0.0333
RFI	0.0027	−0.0714	−0.0050	0.0468
EN	0.1626	0.0893	0.0353	0.0535
DEN	−0.0092	0.0036	−0.0020	0.0021
LIT	0.0376	0.1829	0.0082	0.1095
ALF	−0.5252	−0.0644	−0.1140	−0.0386
HB	0.0006	0.00	0.0001	0.00

[a] *Source*: Tables C17 and C18 of Appendix C.

(*ALF*). However, in the 1970s literacy has taken its place. This would seem to suggest that the differential rates of saving propensities between different socio-economic classes (since these classes are often accompanied by differences in educational attainments) are becoming more important than the rural-urban dichotomy which dominated the 1960s. On the other hand, both periods share the common characteristic, namely, that factors other than the capital inflows are the most dominant ones.

(2) For the growth rate, in the 1960s structural changes and capital accumulation played the most significant role. In the 1970s, while capital accumulation continued to be important, literacy took over the place of structural change as the most significant variable. The results for the growth rate are thus consistent with the findings for the savings rate.

From the above discussion, the most significant observation that we can draw is that in the 1970s, unlike the 1960s while foreign capital inflows exerted a more positive effect on growth and a less dampening effect on the savings rate, they still continued to be outranked by domestic factors. The increasingly important role of investment in human capital is also noteworthy.

CHAPTER VIII

STABILITY ANALYSIS

In the previous chapters, we have developed a simultaneous equations model to explain the behaviour of savings and growth in the developing countries. Using cross-section data, we have estimated the model for two time periods, that is, 1960s and the 1970s. We have also classified or disaggregated our cross-section aggregate sample for 1970s on the basis of per capita income (three income groups) as well as on the basis of geographic regions (three regional groups). We have observed that the estimated coefficients differ between time periods as well as from one group to the other corresponding to any particular scheme of classification. But, these observed differences may be due to chance and therefore may not reflect differences in the underlying population parameters. We, therefore, need to perform some formal tests of stability to ensure that the observed differences in the estimated coefficients reflect true structural differences. Since our purpose in this research is to analyse the behaviour of savings and growth in the developing countries, we will perform stability tests on those two relationships only. In carrying out our stability analysis, we will concern ourselves with the following cases:

(a) the stability of the estimated coefficients over two time period, that is, 1960s and the 1970s;

(b) stability of the coefficients when the sample size is increased;

(c) stability of the coefficients over three income groups; and

(d) stability of the coefficients over three geographical regions.

In Section 1 we will discuss the test procedure. In Section 2, the test procedure outlined in Section 1 will be applied to investigate the stability of the estimated coefficient of the savings rate equation and in Section 3, that of the growth rate equation.

1. AN OUTLINE OF THE TEST PROCEDURE

We propose to perform the Chow [12] test in each of the above cases. The basic problem in the stability analysis is to see whether the two samples from which the coefficients are estimated actually do come from the same population or alternatively, whether they do come from two different populations.

In the former case, we say that the coefficients are not changing from one sample to the other and in the latter case, we say that the coefficients are changing from one sample to the other or in other words, they are different.

To illustrate, let there be two samples with n_1 and n_2 observations, respectively. We can estimate any relationship given by, say,

$$(1) \quad Y = \beta_0 + \beta_1 X_1 + \ldots + \beta_k X_k + u \, ,$$

separately for both samples. The regression equations to be estimated becomes:

$$(2) \quad y = \beta_0^{(1)} + \beta_1^{(1)} X_1 + \ldots + \beta_k X_k^{(1)} + u \, ,$$

$$(3) \quad Y = \beta_0^{(1)} + \beta_1^{(2)} X_1 + \ldots + \beta_k^{(2)} X_k + u \, .$$

The superscripts refer to the corresponding sample group. We want to see whether the β_i coefficients are significantly different between the two samples. Thus, the null hypotheses to be tested becomes:

$$(4) \quad H_0 : \beta_0^{(1)} = \beta_0^{(2)}, \beta_1^{(1)} = \beta_1^{(2)}, = \ldots, \beta_k^{(1)} = \beta_k^{(2)} \, ,$$

against the alternative hypotheses:

$$(5) \quad H_i : \beta_0^{(1)} \neq \beta_0^{(2)}, \beta_1^{(1)} \neq \beta_1^{(2)}, \ldots, \beta_k^{(1)} \neq \beta_k^{(2)} \, .$$

Under the assumption that the null hypotheses are true (Equation (4)), we can estimate Equation (1) from pooled sample and we can then proceed to perform the F-test suggested by Chow.[1] The Chow test, in fact, is nothing more than a test based on a set of linear restrictions, the restrictions being given by Equation (4), where $(k + 1)$ linear restrictions are specified.[2] In the two group case, the F statistic is given as follows:

$$(6) \quad F^* = \frac{[\Sigma e_p^2 - \{\Sigma e_1^2 + \Sigma e_2^2\}]/K}{[(\Sigma e_1^2 + \Sigma e_2^2)/(n_1 + n_2 - 2K)]} \, ,$$

with $\nu_1 = K$ and $\nu_2 = (n_1 + n_2 - 2K)$ degrees of freedom; where

F^* = is the calculated value of F;

Σe_p^2 = ss. residuals from the pooled sample with $(n_1 + n_2 - K)$ degrees of freedom;

Σe_1^2 = ss. residuals from the 1st sample with $(n_1 - K)$ degrees of freedom;

Σe_2^2 = ss. residuals from the 2nd sample with $(n_2 - K)$ degrees of freedom;

K = number of parameters estimated including the constant term; n_1 and n_2 are the sample sizes corresponding to the two samples.

Let F^T be the theoretical value of F (at some chosen level of significance, for example, 5% or 1%) with $\nu_1 = K$ and $\nu_2 = (n_1 + n_2 - 2K)$ degrees of freedom, if the null hypothesis were true. If $F^* > F^T$, we tend to reject the null hypothesis at the chosen level of significance in which case we accept that the two functions differ significantly from one sample to the other. In the opposite case ($F^* < F^T$), we cannot reject the null hypothesis that the coefficient from the two samples are stable.

In the case of three sample groups, the F^* value given by Equation (6) takes the form;

$$(7) \quad F^* = \frac{[\Sigma e_p^2 - \{(\Sigma e_1^2 + \Sigma e_2^2 + \Sigma e_3^2)\}]/2K}{[(\Sigma e_1^2 + \Sigma e_2^2 + \Sigma e_3^2)/(n_1 + n_2 + n_3 - 3K)]},$$

with $\nu_1 = 2K$ and $\nu_2 = (n_1 + n_2 + n_3 - 3K)$ degrees of freedom.[3]

2. THE STABILITY OF THE SAVINGS RATE EQUATION

To test the stability of the coefficients of our estimated savings function we performed the Chow test on the following specification of the savings function:

$$(8) \quad \left(\frac{S}{Y}\right) = \alpha_0 + \alpha_1 \left(\frac{Y}{P}\right) + \alpha_2 G + \alpha_3 DR + \alpha_4 (AID) + \alpha_5 (FPI) + \alpha_6 (RFI).$$

A. *Intertemporal Stability*

We will examine the stability of the estimated coefficients over the two time periods, that is, 1960s and the 1970s. We have relevant data to estimate the savings function with 40 observations for 1960s and 52 observations for th 1970s and together they give 92 (40 + 52) observations for the pooled sample. The summary of the different tests are reported in Table VIII.1. Row (1) of this table gives the test results corresponding to the intertemporal stability. From the 1st row, we find that the calculated value of $F(F^* = 2.2031)$ is greater than the theoretical F value ($F^T_{\alpha = 0.05} = 2.12$) with $\nu_1 = 7$ and $\nu_2 = 78$ degrees of freedom. The F^* value has been calculated using Equation (6) above. Given that $F^* > F^T$, we reject the null hypothesis that the coefficient estimates are stable over time.

TABLE VIII.1.
Summary results of the different tests performed on the stability of the savings rate equation

Tests	F^*	Degrees of freedom	$F_\alpha^T = 0.05$ ($F_\alpha^T = 0.01$)	Result of the test: Accept/Reject null hypothesis
	(1)	(2)	(3)	(4)
(1) Intertemporal stability	2.2031 [a]	$V_1 = 7$ $V_2 = 78$	2.12 (2.87)	Reject
(2) Stability when the sample size is increased	2.0078	$V_1 = 12$ $V_2 = 33$	2.06 (2.78)	Accept
(3) Stability over income groups	2.846 [b]	$V_1 = 14$ $V_2 = 31$	2.03 (2.72)	Reject
(4) Stability over geographic regions	3.0840 [a]	$V_1 = 14$ $V_2 = 28$	2.06 (2.80)	Reject

Note: (i) F^* is the calculated value of F.
(ii) F^T is the theoretical value of F under the assumption that the null hypothesis ($b_i = B_i$) is true. Two alternative values of F^T are reported in col. 3 corresponding to the different levels of significance. The F^T values in the bracket correspond to 1% level of significance.
(iii) [a] Represents significance at $\alpha = 0.05$.
[b] Represents significance at $\alpha = 0.01$.

B. *Stability of the Coefficients When the Sample Size Is Increased*

We have 52 observations for the 1970s out of which 40 countries directly correspond to the sample used by Gupta [33]. The purpose of the test here is to examine the stability of the coefficient estimates as the sample size increases from 40 to 52 observations. The result of this test is reported in the 2nd row of Table VIII.1. where the test suggests that we accept the null hypothesis, that is the coefficients estimated from the augmented sample are not different from that of the original sample. In spite of this result, we worked with 52 observations mainly because the larger sample was useful in having enough degrees of freedom for our estimates in the context of subgroups of the aggregate sample.

C. *Stability of the Savings Function over Income Groups*

We have divided our sample of 52 countries into three income groups in the previous chapters. The results of the regressions corresponding to three income groups are also reported accordingly. We observed that the estimated coefficients differ widely from one group to another in terms of the magnitude and the level of significance of the coefficient estimates. The purpose of the Chow test is to investigate whether these differences are statistically significant.

In this case, the relevant F^* value has been calculated using Equation (7) in Section 1. The test result appears in row 3 of Table VIII.1., where we are able to reject the null hypothesis even at 1% level of significance. In other words, we conclude that the estimated coefficients from three income groups are drawn from three different populations and that the disaggregation on the basis of income in a cross-country study is a meaningful scheme of classification to follow.

D. *Stability of the Savings Function over Geographic Regions*

Similar analysis as in (c) above is carried out for three geographic regions. Again, on the basis of the Chow test, we are able to reject the null hypothesis at the 5% level of significance (Row 4 of Table VIII.1.), that is, that the coefficients estimated from three different geographic regions are significantly different.

3. THE STABILITY OF THE GROWTH RATE EQUATION

To test the stability of the estimated coefficients of the growth rate equation, we again performed Chow test on the following specification of the growth equation:

$$G = \beta_0 + \beta_1 \left(\frac{S}{Y}\right) + \beta_2 (AID) + \beta_3 (FPI) + \beta_4 (RFI) + \beta_5 (GL). \qquad (9)$$

A. *Intertemporal Stability*

As in the case of the savings function, we have also estimated the growth function using data separately on 40 countries for the 1960s and 52 countries [including the above 40 countries] for the 1970s. The result of this test is given in the 1st row of Table VIII.2. where we find that $F^* < F^T$ with appropriate degrees of freedom and the level of significance. Therefore, we

TABLE VIII.2.
Summary results of the different tests performed on the stability of the growth rate equation

Tests	$F^*_{\alpha=0.0}$	Degrees of freedom	$F^T_{\alpha=0.05}$ ($F^T_{\alpha=0.01}$)	Result of the test: Accept/Reject (null hypothesis)
	(1)	(2)	(3)	(4)
(1) Intertemporal stability	1.4697	$V_1 = 6$ $V_2 = 80$	2.21 (3.04)	Accept
(2) Stability when the sample size is increased	1.8184	$V_1 = 12$ $V_2 = 34$	2.05 (2.76)	Accept
(3) Stability over income groups	2.0825 [a]	$V_1 = 12$ $V_2 = 34$	2.05 (2.76)	Reject
(4) Stability over geographic regions	2.2643 [a]	$V_1 = 12$ $V_2 = 31$	2.08 (2.82)	Reject

Note: (i) F^* is the calculated value of F.
(ii) F^T is the theoretical value of F under the null hypothesis ($b_i = B_i$). Two alternative values of F^T are reported in col. 3 corresponding to two different levels of significance (the value in the bracket represents 1% level of significance).
(ii) [a] Represents significance at $\alpha = 0.05$.
[b] Represents significance at $\alpha = 0.01$.

were unable to reject the null hypotheses in the case of the growth function [the null hypotheses were rejected in the case of the savings function], or in other words, the coefficients of the growth function were not very much different between 1960s and 1970s. Such similarity was also reported by Papanek[4] for his growth equation for the 1950s and the 1960s as well. Papanek did not use the Chow test, but he used an almost equivalent test called Dummy variable test to distinguish the two time periods, 1950s and 1960s. The two tests can be shown equivalent[5] because both the unrestricted (from separate groups) and the restricted (from the pooled sample) residual sums of squares can be obtained from the same dummy variable regression if enough Dummy-variables are introduced.[6]

B. *The Stability of the Coefficients When the Sample Size Is Increased*

Like the savings function, we have also tested whether the coefficient estimates of the growth equation remain stable when the size of the sample is increased from 40 to 52 observations. Row 2 of Table VIII.2. supports that we do not reject the null hypotheses ($F^* < F^T_{\alpha = 0.05}$) at the 5% level of significance.

C. *Stability of the Growth Function Over Income Groups*

In Chapter II, Table 1, we have found that the mean and the standard deviations of the growth rate for three income groups are different from each other. In Chapter III, Table 8 we further observed that the estimated regression coefficients were also different in terms of the magnitude as well as the level of significance of the coefficients. We want to investigate whether these differences are statistically significant. The relevant test result is reported in the 3rd row of Table VIII.2. and we find that $F^* > F^T_{\alpha = 0.05}$ with $\nu_1 = 12$ and $\nu_2 = 34$ degrees of freedom. This implies that we cannot accept the null hypothesis, or alternatively, the three income groups give statistically significant differences in the estimated coefficients. Thus, the coefficients estimated from a highly aggregated sample may not be representative of the true state of affairs. This result is parallel to that found for the stability analysis of the savings function as well. Unfortunately, many cross section studies, including that of Papanek, Stoneman, Weisskopf and others failed to recognize that disaggregation on the basis of per capita income may provide useful information about the growth patterns of developing countries.

D. *The Stability of the Growth Function Over Geographic Regions*

The relevant test result is reported in the 4th row of Table VIII.2., which indicates a rejection of the null hypotheses at the 5% level of significance with degrees of freedom 12 and 31 respectively for the numerator and the denominator. Geographic differences have been recognized by many authors including Papanek, Galbraith, among others. Papanek found significant regional differences in his regression coefficients but he did not perform any formal test of stability over the classified groups. To quote Papanek,

> The results of disaggregation by region also suggest another reason why some analyses of the effect of savings, aid, or total resource inflows on growth have been unsatisfactory. An examination of the relationship which focuses on Latin America or Africa would show little effect of aid or total resource inflows on growth. To draw conclusions for Asia from such analysis would obviously be incorrect.[7]

Galbraith also argues that capital, and specially foreign exchange, are crucial constraints on growth in a number of Asian countries, while political, social and human factors are more important for some countries in Latin America and Africa.[8] Thus, on the basis of our analysis, we can argue that disaggregation of our aggregative sample on the basis of geographic regions provides another meaningful technique to understand and study the growth process of the developing countries.

CHAPTER IX

AGGREGATION AND PREDICTIONS

On the basis of our theoretical framework and empirical estimates in the previous chapters, we have been able to derive some important policy conclusions about the savings and growth patterns in the developing countries. But greater reliance cannot be placed on those results unless our model is capable of explaining the economic facts at least within the sample period. Therefore, in this chapter, we propose to examine the predictive performance of our estimated model within the sample period only. But, in evaluating the predictive performance of our model under alternative classifcatory scheme, we will not attempt to apply any rigorous econometric tests. We will mainly concern ourselves with simple comparisons and casual observations. Further, outside the sample forecasts will not be attempted either becuase of data constraints or because they are not the major concern of this study. In addition, our analysis of predictions will be limited to two endogenous variables only. These are the rate of savings and the rate of growth of GNP, respectively.

This chapter will be divided into three main sections. In Section 1, we will discuss predictions of the savings rate followed by predictions of the growth rate in Section 2, for each country under different classification schemes. In Section 3, we will make some comments on the methodology of classifying countries as 'overachievers' and 'underachievers'[1] and their implications for different level and type of sample aggregation in a cross-section world. In the case of all these three sections, we will analyse the sensitivity of the results with respect to: (i) the form of the estimated equation used (i.e., structural equation vs. reduced form equation); and (ii) the level and type of sample disaggregation. Two types of sample disaggregation will be considered as before: (a) sample disaggregation on the basis of per capita income and (b) sample disaggregation on the basis of geographical regions.

1. THE SAVINGS RATE PREDICTIONS

The within sample predictions on the savings rate were carried out using both the structural equation and the reduced form equation and the predicted values were derived for each country in the context of all different types of sample disaggregation, e.g., total sample as well as different subgroups of the total sample. The actual saving rate is given in Column (1) of Table IX.1. Columns (2) and (3) give predictions from the structural equation (reported in Chapter VI) and the reduced form equation (reported in Chapter VII), respectively. Corresponding results for the three income groups are given in columns (1) to (3) of Tables IX.2. to IX.4. whereas those for the geographical regions are reported in columns (1) to (3) of Tables IX.5. to IX.7.

A careful examination of all these results suggests the following: (a) predictions based on structural equation performs better than that based on reduced form equation, irrespective of the level and type of sample disaggregation; (b) the predictions derived on the basis of sample disaggregation (either on the basis of income or on the basis of geographic regions) were found to be better than that based on aggregate sample. This holds true irrespective of whether the structural equation or the reduced form of the model is used in deriving the predicted values. The evidence in support of the above two points are further strengthened when we consider Table IX.8.,

TABLE IX.1.
Actual and predicted values of the saving and growth rates: Predicted from total sample

SL. No.	Country	Actual saving rate (1)	Predicted saving rate from structural equation (2)	Predicted saving rate from reduced form (3)	Actual growth rate (4)	Predicted growth rate from structural equation (5)	Predicted growth rate from reduced form (6)
1.	Afghanistan	1.60	15.09	12.59	3.20	2.48	5.35
2.	Algeria	28.10	25.75	15.37	7.00	7.85	4.51
3.	Argentina	19.40	22.04	15.86	4.50	5.92	4.99
4.	Bolivia	14.60	14.07	9.94	4.90	6.09	4.86
5.	Brazil	15.90	24.79	14.99	9.00	5.95	5.71
6.	Burma	9.80	13.80	14.52	3.00	4.92	6.15
7.	Chad	0.70	13.76	15.04	−0.90	5.09	4.25
8.	Chile	15.60	21.56	19.19	3.30	4.66	5.60
9.	Colombia	17.60	19.04	13.41	6.10	6.64	5.54
10.	Costa Rica	16.10	19.28	13.80	6.80	7.28	6.68
11.	Cyprus	16.90	17.52	9.59	7.40	7.92	6.01
12.	Dom. Rep.	9.60	19.43	11.33	8.40	6.23	6.68
13.	Ecuador	13.80	18.88	14.82	6.00	6.57	6.83
14.	Egypt	7.80	16.99	12.26	3.30	2.65	3.82
15.	El Salvador	12.60	21.59	17.65	4.60	4.07	5.39
16.	Ethiopia	12.10	17.32	12.60	4.20	4.08	4.21

Table IX.1. (continued)

SL. No.	Country	Actual saving rate (1)	Predicted saving rate from structural equation (2)	Predicted saving rate from reduced form (3)	Actual growth rate (4)	Predicted growth rate from structural equation (5)	Predicted growth rate from reduced form (6)
17.	Ghana	11.60	16.43	14.52	3.50	5.36	6.12
18.	Greece	18.40	24.63	12.01	8.00	5.47	3.79
19.	Guatemala	11.70	23.12	16.42	6.10	4.32	5.56
20.	Guyana	15.60	13.97	11.67	2.60	6.63	5.60
21.	Hondurus	12.40	13.18	11.94	4.10	7.14	7.02
22.	India	14.40	17.73	14.62	3.50	4.31	4.36
23.	Indonesia	9.20	21.02	14.79	6.80	3.69	5.15
24.	Iran	16.80	31.03	18.36	11.30	6.19	6.60
25.	Iraq	21.20	25.94	18.26	5.90	6.34	5.57
26.	Israel	6.40	21.54	8.78	9.70	7.32	7.94
27.	Ivory Coast	18.70	21.84	15.20	7.40	6.89	5.97
28.	Jamaica	17.40	20.46	15.63	6.10	7.13	6.66
29.	Kenya	18.40	20.35	15.73	7.10	7.90	7.20
30.	Korea (Rep.)	16.30	19.60	11.02	10.90	8.52	7.13
31.	Lebanon	15.60	22.56	14.51	6.20	5.26	4.97
32.	Malaysia	20.70	23.57	17.96	5.80	5.85	5.13
33.	Malta	14.50	16.96	10.44	7.40	7.51	6.45
34.	Mexico	16.10	22.08	13.97	6.50	5.65	5.09
35.	Morocco	10.00	17.79	11.70	4.90	4.83	5.27
36.	Nicaragua	12.20	18.14	12.49	4.50	4.90	4.97
37.	Pakistan	13.60	20.57	16.18	5.30	5.07	5.74
38.	Panama	21.10	25.91	19.64	7.60	7.54	7.17
39.	Paraguay	11.40	18.52	12.63	5.10	4.24	4.56
40.	Peru	15.80	19.00	15.08	4.70	5.90	5.71
41.	Philippines	18.50	20.57	17.39	5.80	6.71	6.42
42.	Portugal	17.00	22.51	13.07	6.50	5.49	4.45
43.	Saudi Arabia	31.60	33.61	15.56	12.70	8.81	4.61
44.	Spain	21.40	33.26	14.46	6.30	6.46	4.65
45.	Sri Lanka	15.70	13.21	10.58	4.20	6.14	4.80
46.	Tanzania	17.90	17.98	12.68	5.30	5.91	4.54
47.	Thailand	20.20	20.81	13.45	7.40	6.76	4.99
48.	Trinidad-Tobago	19.60	24.53	20.50	3.80	4.66	4.90
49.	Turkey	20.40	21.49	13.99	6.60	6.10	4.42
50.	Uruguay	10.40	16.00	14.91	1.40	3.27	4.45
51.	Venezuala	25.40	22.51	16.23	4.50	8.48	6.08
52.	Japan	40.60	37.01	18.54	10.80	10.58	4.81

TABLE IX.2.
Actual and predicted values of the saving and growth rates: predicted from income group I

SL. No.	Country	Actual saving rate (1)	Predicted saving rate from structural equation (2)	Predicted saving rate from reduced form (3)	Actual growth rate (4)	Predicted growth rate from structural equation (5)	Predicted growth rate from reduced form (6)
1.	Afghanistan	1.60	7.82	10.73	3.20	1.74	4.24
4.	Bolivia	14.60	14.97	7.52	4.90	4.69	3.93
6.	Burma	9.80	11.93	11.89	3.00	3.61	4.52
7.	Chad	0.70	0.25	8.11	−0.90	1.28	3.24
14.	Egypt	7.80	8.08	13.45	3.30	2.20	5.00
16.	Ethiopia	12.10	13.04	9.28	4.20	3.76	3.29
17.	Ghana	11.60	12.01	14.66	3.50	4.87	6.58
22.	India	14.40	11.93	10.23	3.50	4.19	4.43
23.	Indonesia	9.20	13.32	12.84	6.80	4.71	6.40
29.	Kenya	18.40	16.70	16.89	7.10	7.24	7.67
37.	Pakistan	13.60	10.31	12.39	5.30	4.73	5.60
41.	Philippines	18.50	17.67	15.04	5.80	5.70	6.63
45.	Sri Lanka	15.70	10.92	13.54	4.20	5.74	6.43
46.	Tanzania	17.90	14.84	10.77	5.30	5.84	4.43
47.	Thailand	20.20	22.62	15.30	7.40	6.37	6.57

TABLE IX.3.
Actual and predicted values of the saving and growth rates: Predicted from income group II

SL. No.	Country	Actual saving rate (1)	Predicted saving rate from structural equation (2)	Predicted saving rate from reduced form (3)	Actual growth rate (4)	Predicted growth rate from structural equation (5)	Predicted growth rate from reduced form (6)
2.	Algeria	28.10	24.90	24.03	7.00	5.89	4.79
5.	Brazil	15.90	18.56	14.19	9.00	7.07	6.63
9.	Colombia	17.60	13.99	14.79	6.10	7.26	6.54
12.	Dom. Rep.	9.60	11.49	9.68	8.40	6.25	6.52
13.	Ecuador	13.80	11.45	12.95	6.00	6.36	6.18
15.	El Salvador	12.60	12.60	13.25	4.60	5.34	5.97
19.	Guatemala	11.70	14.96	14.41	6.10	4.99	5.86
20.	Guyana	15.60	13.50	13.97	2.60	5.82	5.37
21.	Hondurus	12.40	13.06	14.92	4.10	7.16	7.91
27.	Ivory Coast	18.70	22.37	17.70	7.40	6.29	6.05
30.	Korea (Rep.)	16.30	13.85	9.86	10.90	9.12	8.24

Table IX.3. (continued)

SL. No.	Country	Actual saving rate (1)	Predicted saving rate from structural equation (2)	Predicted saving rate from reduced form (3)	Actual growth rate (4)	Predicted growth rate from structural equation (5)	Predicted growth rate from reduced form (6)
32.	Malaysia	20.70	16.64	15.97	5.80	7.18	5.99
35.	Morocco	10.00	12.92	15.45	4.90	4.51	6.10
36.	Nicaragua	12.20	15.24	16.46	4.50	4.19	5.40
39.	Paraguay	11.40	10.80	13.60	5.10	4.89	5.50
49.	Turkey	20.40	19.48	14.07	6.60	6.81	5.19

TABLE IX.4.

Actual and predicted values of the saving and growth rates: Predicted from income group III

SL. No.	Country	Actual saving rate (1)	Predicted saving rate from structural equation (2)	Predicted saving rate from reduced form (3)	Actual growth rate (4)	Predicted growth rate from structural equation (5)	Predicted growth rate from reduced form (6)
3.	Argentina	19.40	19.57	17.13	4.50	5.71	4.92
8.	Chile	15.60	12.53	15.24	3.30	6.24	6.12
10.	Costa Rica	16.10	14.25	13.09	6.80	6.98	5.93
11.	Cyprus	16.90	12.01	8.53	7.40	8.54	5.61
18.	Greece	18.40	20.51	13.88	8.00	6.31	4.73
24.	Iran	16.80	18.63	14.75	11.30	8.10	7.38
25.	Iraq	21.20	22.57	22.69	5.90	5.46	5.99
26.	Israel	6.40	11.93	8.90	9.70	8.76	6.52
28.	Jamaica	17.40	19.65	20.18	6.10	6.04	7.02
31.	Lebanon	15.60	18.49	16.42	6.20	5.04	5.33
33.	Malta	14.50	12.99	11.27	7.40	6.95	5.82
34.	Mexico	16.10	18.06	14.95	6.50	5.60	5.20
38.	Panama	21.10	19.05	17.77	7.60	8.02	6.85
40.	Peru	15.80	14.24	15.88	4.70	5.33	5.37
42.	Portugal	17.00	15.58	13.19	6.50	7.01	5.68
43.	Saudi Arabia	31.60	31.00	21.53	12.70	8.95	5.43
44.	Spain	21.40	20.52	16.08	6.30	6.63	4.77
48.	Trinidad-Tobago	19.60	24.24	25.16	3.80	3.15	5.11
50.	Urugay	10.40	13.62	17.35	1.40	2.19	4.63
51.	Venezuela	25.40	19.34	16.10	4.50	8.95	5.69
52.	Japan	40.60	38.14	21.69	10.80	11.36	4.74

TABLE IX.5.
Actual and predicted values of the saving and growth rates: Predicted from geographic region – Asia

SL. No.	Country	Actual saving rate (1)	Predicted saving rate from structural equation (2)	form (3)	Actual growth rate (4)	Predicted growth rate from structural equation (5)	reduced form (6)
1.	Afghanistan	1.60	8.87	11.56	3.20	1.72	5.21
6.	Burma	9.80	12.45	19.43	3.00	4.36	7.74
11.	Cyprus	16.90	14.62	11.06	7.40	8.42	6.37
22.	India	14.40	15.44	13.63	3.50	3.87	3.60
23.	Indonesia	9.20	10.60	11.51	6.80	6.07	6.88
24.	Iran	16.80	17.21	20.86	11.30	11.21	12.64
25.	Iraq	21.20	19.54	23.92	5.90	6.53	7.49
26.	Israel	6.40	10.85	8.86	9.70	8.60	9.46
30.	Korea (Rep.)	16.30	14.59	12.75	10.90	10.38	9.14
31.	Lebanon	15.60	14.72	15.58	6.20	4.95	4.94
32.	Malaysia	20.70	19.81	24.48	5.80	5.67	6.99
37.	Pakistan	13.60	12.93	19.15	5.30	6.56	8.51
41.	Philippines	18.50	19.15	27.59	5.80	7.39	10.58
43.	Saudi	31.60	34.21	18.32	12.70	9.23	4.58
45.	Sri Lanka	15.70	5.80	3.11	4.20	6.46	2.05
47.	Thailand	20.20	21.82	15.22	7.40	6.97	5.22
49.	Turkey	20.40	19.90	12.28	6.60	6.33	3.48
52.	Japan	40.60	37.55	25.12	10.80	11.82	6.39

TABLE IX.6.
Actual and predicted values of the saving and growth rates: Predicted from Geographic Region – Africa

SL. No.	Country	Actual saving rate (1)	Predicted saving rate from structural equation (2)	reduced form (3)	Actual growth rate (4)	Predicted growth rate from structural equation (5)	reduced form (6)
2.	Algeria	28.10	26.42	27.98	7.00	7.30	8.13
7.	Chad	0.70	1.19	8.93	–0.09	–0.06	1.88
4.	Egypt	7.80	8.91	13.38	3.30	2.94	5.09
6.	Ethiopia	12.10	11.63	5.53	4.20	4.08	2.15
7.	Ghana	11.60	10.05	19.22	3.50	4.58	7.20
7.	Ivory Coast	18.70	22.78	15.31	7.40	6.10	5.42
9.	Kenya	18.40	17.47	14.08	7.10	7.15	6.10
3.	Malta	14.50	13.96	17.38	7.40	7.63	10.18
5.	Morocco	10.00	12.41	12.95	4.90	4.19	5.44
6.	Tanzania	17.90	15.18	6.08	5.30	5.80	2.32

TABLE IX.7.
Actual and predicted values of the saving and growth rates: Predicted from geographic region – Latin America

SL. Country No.	Actual saving rate (1)	Predicted saving rate from structural equation (2)	reduced form (3)	Actual growth rate (4)	Predicted growth rate from structural equation (5)	reduced form (6)
3. Argentina	19.40	21.19	15.32	4.50	4.62	4.98
4. Bolivia	14.60	14.77	15.90	4.90	4.23	4.27
5. Brazil	15.90	16.25	13.73	9.00	5.47	5.41
8. Chile	15.60	17.77	18.43	3.30	4.30	4.38
9. Colombia	17.60	13.10	14.05	6.10	5.35	5.24
0. Costa Rica	16.10	14.55	14.46	6.80	6.44	6.40
2. Dom. Rep.	9.60	13.89	11.42	8.40	6.59	6.66
3. Ecuador	13.80	12.76	13.99	6.00	6.44	6.45
5. El salvador	12.60	12.37	11.90	4.60	4.93	4.95
9. Guatemala	11.70	14.43	12.48	6.10	5.15	5.19
0. Guyana	15.60	12.41	11.39	2.60	5.59	5.47
1. Hondurms	12.40	11.30	12.91	4.10	6.91	6.93
8. Jamica	17.40	17.49	14.08	6.10	5.87	5.82
4. Mexico	16.10	16.76	14.25	6.50	4.80	4.75
6. Nicaragua	12.20	14.69	13.51	4.50	4.56	4.60
8. Panama	21.10	19.36	17.26	7.60	6.27	6.16
9. Paraguay	11.40	12.74	14.04	5.10	4.19	4.26
0. Peru	15.80	13.41	13.64	4.70	5.57	5.50
8. Trinidad-Tobago	19.60	17.54	14.67	3.80	4.07	3.97
0. Uruguay	10.40	14.51	14.63	1.40	3.91	4.05
1. Venezuala	25.40	22.18	14.72	4.50	5.98	5.67

columns (1) and (2), which report the value of simple correlation coefficient between the actual and the predicted values of savings rate on the basis of all different types of sample groups as well as the different form of the estimated equation used. If we compare columns (1) and (2) of Table IX.8., we find support for our first observation, that is, that in all cases of sample disaggregation, the correlation coefficient is higher when the structural equation is used than when the reduced form equation is used. With regard to our second observation, we find that irrespective of the form of the equation used (i.e., structural equation or reduced form equation) the correlation coefficient in all cases of sample disaggregation (income groups or regional groups) is higher than that of the aggregate sample. This result is expected given that the

TABLE IX.8.
Simple correlation coefficient between actual and predicted values of saving and growth rates on the basis of sample groups and the form of equation used

Level and type of sample disaggregation	Simple correlation coefficient between actual and predicted values			
	Saving rate		Growth rate	
	From structural Equation (1)	From reduced form Equation (2)	From structural Equation (3)	From reduced form Equation (4)
Total sample	0.74	0.41	0.70	0.32
Income groups				
I	0.87	0.48	0.82	0.67
II	0.83	0.67	0.61	0.42
III	0.91	0.61	0.76	0.30
Regional groups				
Asia	0.92	0.50	0.89	0.36
Africa	0.96	0.57	0.97	0.61
Latin America	0.78	0.47	0.50	0.50

grouping procedure allows the countries within a particular group to be more homogeneous and thus enables the model to provide better predictive performance.[2] But, from Table IX.8., we cannot suggest which type of classifications scheme is superior, geographic or income groups.

To make further comparisons, we have prepared the summary Table IX.9., columns (1) to (4), which combines the results of different sample groups into one table. In this table, column (1) gives actual savings rate, column (2) gives predicted savings rate from total sample, columns (3) and (4) report predicted values derived from appropriate income group and appropriate geographic group, respectively. We can now resort to country by country comparison of the predictive performance. Comparing columns (1), (2) and (3) of this table, we observe that in the case of 40 out of 52 countries (77%), the grouping on the basis of income gave predicted value closer to the actual value whereas, the aggregate sample gave closer value only in the case of 12 countries (23%). Similar comparisons of columns (1), (2) and (4) reveal that geographic grouping gave closer predicted value in 81% of the cases (42 countries) compared to 19% cases (10 countries) in which aggregate sample gave closer predictions. Thus, we can conclude that, on the whole, disaggregation of the total sample either on the basis of income or geographic region provides us with better predictive performance.

Finally, let us compare columns (1), (3) and (4) to see the relative performance of income grouping vis-à-vis geographic grouping. We find that geographic grouping provided closer predicted value in 65% cases compared to total sample whereas, income grouping gave closer predictions in 35% cases.

Thus, on the basis of our limited analysis in this section, we come to the following three tentative conclusions:

(a) Predictions based on structural equation performs better than that based on reduced form equation, irrespective of the level and the type of sample disaggregation made.

(b) Irrespective of the form of the equation used (structural equation or reduced form equation), the predictions based on sample disaggregation (either on the basis of income or geographic region) performs much better than the aggregate sample.

(c) Predictions based on geographic grouping performs slightly better than grouping based on per capita income.

2. THE GROWTH RATE PREDICTIONS

A very similar analysis was carried out on growth rate predictions as was done in the case of savings rate in the previous section. As before, we used both the structural equation and the reduced form equation. The same pattern of sample disaggregation into income groups and geographic eegions was followed. Columns (4) to (6) of Table IX.1. report the results on predictions corresponding to the aggregate sample, Tables IX.2., IX.3., and IX.4. correspond to three income groups and Tables IX.5., IX.6., and IX.7. represent three geographic regions.

The three tentative conclusions reached in the case of saving rate predictions also hold in the case of growth rate predictions. A casual observation of these results reveal that: (a) irrespective of the level and type of sample disaggregation, predictions of growth rate based on structural equation performed better than those based on the reduced form equation; (b) irrespective of the form of the equation used in deriving predicted value of growth rates, predictions on the basis of sample disaggregation is much better than the predictions on the basis of the aggregate sample. Further support in favour of these two observations are available from Table IX.8. which gives correlation coefficient between actual and the predicted values of growth rate. Comparing columns (3) and (4) of this table, we find that these coefficients are higher when the structural equation is used compared to the reduced form equation. This holds in all cases of the sample disaggregation with the exception of income group II and the Latin American sample when the structural equation is used or in the case of income group III when reduced form equation is used. Thus, in the case of growth rate predictions also, the disaggregated sample performed better than aggregate sample, independent of the form of the equation used in deriving predicted values. Again, as in the case of savings rate predictions, we cannot say anything about the relative performance of the income groups vis-à-vis geographic groups from Table IX.8. alone.

For further comparison, we again refer to summary Table IX.9. In this table, column (5) reports actual growth rate by country, column (6) gives predicted value of growth rate based on aggregate sample, columns (7) and (8) give, respectively, the predicted values derived from appropriate income groups and appropriate geographic regions. A country by country comparison reveals the following: (i) in 31 out of 52 cases (60%) disaggregation on the basis of income resulted in closer predicted values than that given by aggregate sample. The opposite is true in 21 cases (40%). This result is derived by comparing columns (5), (6) and (7) of Table IX.9. (ii) Comparing columns (5), (6) and (8), we find that in 63% cases, regional grouping performed better than aggregate sample, in 37% cases otherwise. (iii) If we compare columns (5), (7) and (8), we observe that a geographic grouping has a slight

TABLE IX.9.
Actual and predicted values of savings and growth rates: Comparison of predictive performance from total sample and two group models[a]

Country	Actual saving rate (1)	Predicted saving rate: From total sample (2)	Predicted saving rate: From app. income group (3)	Predicted saving rate: From app. geog. group (4)	Actual growth rate (5)	Predicted growth rate: From total sample (6)	Predicted growth rate: From app. income group (7)	Predicted growth rate: From app. geog. group (8)
Afghanistan	1.60	15.09	7.82	8.87	3.20	2.48	1.74	1.72
Algeria	28.10	25.75	24.90	26.42	7.00	7.85	5.89	7.30
Argentina	19.40	22.04	19.57	21.19	4.50	5.92	5.71	4.62
Bolivia	14.60	14.07	14.97	14.77	4.90	6.09	4.69	4.23
Brazil	15.90	24.79	18.56	16.25	9.00	5.95	7.07	5.47
Burma	9.80	13.80	11.93	12.45	3.00	4.92	3.61	4.36
Chad	0.70	13.76	0.25	1.19	−0.90	5.09	1.28	−0.06
Chile	15.60	21.56	12.53	17.77	3.30	4.66	6.24	4.30
Colombia	17.60	19.04	13.99	13.10	6.10	6.64	7.26	5.35
Costa Rica	16.10	19.28	14.25	14.55	6.80	7.28	6.98	6.44
Cyprus	16.90	17.52	12.01	14.62	7.40	7.92	8.54	8.42
Dom. Rep.	9.60	19.43	11.49	13.89	8.40	6.23	6.25	6.59
Korea (R.)	16.30	19.60	13.85	14.59	10.90	8.52	9.12	10.38
Lebanon	15.60	22.56	18.49	14.72	6.20	5.26	5.04	4.95
Malaysia	20.70	23.57	16.64	19.81	5.80	5.85	7.18	5.67
Malta	14.50	16.96	12.99	13.96	7.40	7.51	6.95	7.63
Mexico	16.10	22.08	18.06	16.76	6.50	5.65	5.60	4.80
Morocco	10.00	17.79	12.92	12.41	4.90	4.83	4.51	4.19
Nicaragua	12.20	18.14	15.24	14.69	4.50	4.90	4.19	4.56
Pakistan	13.60	20.57	10.31	12.93	5.30	5.07	4.73	6.56
Panama	21.10	25.91	19.05	19.36	7.60	7.54	8.02	6.27
Paraguay	11.40	18.52	10.80	12.74	5.10	4.24	4.89	4.19
Peru	15.80	19.00	14.24	13.41	4.70	5.90	5.33	5.57

Table IX.9. (continued)

Country	(1)	(2)	(3)	(4)	(5)	(6)	(7)	(8)
Philippines	18.50	20.57	17.67	19.15	5.80	6.71	5.70	7.39
Portugal	17.00	22.51	15.58	–	6.50	5.49	7.01	–
Saudi Arabia	31.60	33.61	31.00	34.21	12.70	8.81	8.95	9.23
Spain	21.40	23.26	20.52	–	6.30	6.46	6.63	–
Sri Lanka	15.70	13.21	10.92	5.80	4.20	6.14	5.74	6.46
Tanzania	17.90	17.98	14.84	15.18	5.30	5.91	5.84	5.80
Thailand	20.20	20.81	22.62	21.82	7.40	6.76	6.37	6.97
Ecuador	13.80	18.88	11.45	12.76	6.00	6.57	6.36	6.44
El Salvador	12.60	21.59	13.61	12.37	4.60	4.07	5.34	4.93
Ethiopia	12.10	17.32	13.04	11.63	4.20	4.09	3.76	4.08
Ghana	11.60	16.43	12.01	10.05	3.50	5.36	4.87	4.58
Greece	18.40	24.63	20.51	–	8.00	5.47	6.31	–
Guatemala	11.70	23.12	14.96	14.43	6.10	4.32	4.99	5.15
Guyana	15.60	13.97	13.50	12.41	2.60	6.63	5.82	5.59
Honduras	12.40	13.18	13.06	11.30	4.10	7.14	7.16	6.19
India	14.40	17.73	11.93	15.44	3.50	4.31	4.19	3.87
Indonesia	9.20	21.02	13.32	10.60	6.80	3.69	4.71	6.07
Iran	16.80	31.03	18.63	17.21	11.30	6.19	8.10	11.21
Iraq	21.20	25.94	22.57	19.54	5.90	6.34	5.46	6.53
Israel	6.40	21.54	11.93	10.85	9.70	7.32	8.76	8.60
Ivory Coast	18.70	21.84	22.37	22.78	7.40	6.89	6.29	6.10
Jamaica	17.40	20.46	19.64	17.49	6.10	7.13	6.04	5.87
Kenya	18.40	20.35	16.70	17.47	7.10	7.90	7.24	7.15
Trinidad-Tobago	19.60	24.53	24.24	17.54	3.80	4.66	3.15	4.07
Turkey	20.40	21.49	19.48	19.90	6.60	6.10	6.81	6.33
Uruguay	10.40	16.00	13.62	14.51	1.40	3.27	2.19	3.91
Venezuela	25.40	22.51	19.34	22.18	4.50	8.48	8.95	5.98
Japan	40.60	37.01	38.14	37.55	10.80	10.58	11.36	11.82

[a] *Source*: Tables IX.1–7.

advantage over income grouping i.e., in 56% cases, geographic grouping provided closer predicted value and 44% cases otherwise.

Thus, the three tentative conclusions derived in the context of evaluating predictive performance of the savings rate from our estimated model still hold in the context of growth rate predictions. In any economic analyses dealing with cross-country data, the researcher must always keep in mind the implication of the level of sample aggregation. Ideally, country studies may provide more useful insights, but when dealing with cross-country data, one must attempt appropriate level and type of disaggregation whenever possible to minimize or at least partially reduce the aggregation bias into the analyses.[3]

3. SOME COMMENTS ON THE CLASSIFICATION OF COUNTRIES AS 'OVERACHIEVERS' AND 'UNDERACHIEVERS'

In his 1973 paper [48], Papanek classified some of his sample countries as 'Overachievers' and 'Underachievers' on the basis of the estimated deviations of the predicted growth rate from the actual (observed) growth rate. To quote him, "The countries whose actual growth rate differed substantially from the growth rate predicted by the regression can shed some light on the regression results and on the mechanism of growth".[4] The following countries were classified as 'Overachievers'[5] by Papanek: Taiwan, Japan, Iran, Ivory Coast, Mexico, Panama, Nicaragua, Zambia, Philippines and South Korea. The countries which are identified as 'Underachievers'[6] are: Trinidad-Tobago, Indonesia, Morocco, Uruguay, Argentina, Burma and Ghana.

In this exercise, Papanek used a single-equation model to derive the predicted values of the growth rate for each country. In addition, the regression equation was estimated by using a very highly aggregated cross-section sample of countries. In our previous chapters, we have persuasively argued that a simultaneous equation approach is to be preferred over single-equation approach in analysing growth and savings patterns in the developing countries. We have also argued that the cross-section data should be disaggregated on some appropriate basis while estimating the theoretical relationships. We strongly believe that such disaggregation procedure should be followed in the context of deriving predictions as well. We have already established the validity of this point in the two previous sections of this chapter. In this section, therefore, we propose to examine how far and to what extent the classification of countries as 'Overachievers' and 'Underachievers' are sensitive with respect to

(i) the form of the equation used; and

(ii) the level and type of sample disaggregation vis-à-vis the aggregate sample.

Let 'O' stand for countries identified as 'Overachievers' and 'U' for 'Underachievers'. In Table IX.10., we have listed 12 countries which are found to be 'Overachievers' independent of the type of sample disaggregation or the form of the equation used in deriving predicted values. Out of the 10 countries [7] listed by Papanek as 'Overachievers', only three of them (Ivory Coast, Mexico and South Korea) appear in our list of 'Overachievers'. The remaining five countries are found to be either 'Underachievers' (for example, Nicaragua, see Table IX.11.) or could not be clearly classified (for example, Japan or Taiwan, see Table IX.12.).

Table IX.11. reports the list of 14 countries which are found to be clearly 'Underachievers', i.e., they are 'Underachievers' irrespective of the type of sample disaggregation or the form of equation used. Surprisingly enough, we observe that all the seven countries classified by Papanek as 'Underachievers' during the 1950s and 1960s do appear in our list of 'Underachieving' countries as well. The countries which were 'Underachieving' during the 1950s and 1960s are performing badly even during the seventies! A careful country analysis is required of these countries to determine the causes of their consistent failures.

Most interesting results are reported in Table IX.12. In this table, we have listed 26 countries which cannot be clearly classified as 'Overachievers' or 'Underachievers'. The classification of these countries are found to be very sensitive to: (i) the form of the estimated equation used i.e., results differ depending upon whether structural or the reduced form predictions are considered; and (ii) the level and type of sample disaggregation, i.e., whether predictions are made using data on aggregate sample or whether predictions are carried out using disaggregated sample on the basis of income or geographic regions. Thus, no consistent pattern emerges out of this table. The point that emerges out of the discussion in this section is that one should be careful in making predictions using a single-equation model (in a world where the relationships are simultaneous) and estimating that equation from a sample of non-homogenous countries aggregated into a single homogenous group. What is suggested is that in a cross-country analysis, at least some level of disaggregation on some appropriate basis should always be followed.

TABLE IX.10.
List of the countries which are consistently 'Overachievers' irrespective of the type of sample disaggregation or form of equation used

SL. No.	Country	Structural equation			Reduced form equation		
		From total sample	From appropriate income group	From appropriate geographic region	From total sample	From appropriate income group	From appropriate geographic region
5.	Brazil	O	O	O	O	O	O
12.	Dom. Rep.	O	O	O	O	O	O
18.	Greece	O	O	O	O	O	O
19.	Guatemala	O	O	O	O	O	O
23.	Indonesia	O	O	O	O	O	O
26.	Israel	O	O	O	O	O	O
27.	Ivory Coast	O	O	O	O	O	O
30.	Korea (Rep.)	O	O	O	O	O	O
31.	Lebanon	O	O	O	O	O	O
34.	Mexico	O	O	O	O	O	O
43.	Saudi Arabia	O	O	O	O	O	O
47.	Thailand	O	O	O	O	O	O

Note: Entry 'O' stands for 'Overachievers'.

TABLE IX.11.
List of the countries which are 'Underachievers' consistently, irrespective of the type of sample disaggregation or the form of equation used

SL. No.	Country	Structural equation			Reduced form equation		
		From total sample	From appropriate income group	From appropriate geographic region	From total sample	From appropriate income group	From appropriate geographic region
3.	Argentina	U	U	U	U	U	U
6.	Burma	U	U	U	U	U	U
7.	Chad	U	U	U	U	U	U
8.	Chile	U	U	U	U	U	U
13.	Ecuador	U	U	U	U	U	U
17.	Ghana	U	U	U	U	U	U
20.	Guyana	U	U	U	U	U	U
21.	Hondurus	U	U	U	U	U	U
22.	India	U	U	U	U	U	U
36.	Nicaragua	U	U	U	U	U	U
40.	Peru	U	U	U	U	U	U
48.	Trinidad-Tobago	U	U	U	U	U	U
50.	Uruguay	U	U	U	U	U	U
51.	Venezuala	U	U	U	U	U	U

Note: 'U' stands for 'Underachievers'.

TABLE IX.12.
List of the countries which cannot be clearly classified as either 'Overachievers' [O] or 'Underachievers' (U)

SL. No.	Country	Structural equation			Reduced form equation		
		From total sample	From appropriate income group	From appropriate geographic region	From total sample	From appropriate income group	From appropriate geographic region
1.	Afghanistan	O	O	O	U	U	U
2.	Algeria	U	O	U	O	O	U
4.	Bolivia	U	O	O	O	O	O
9.	Colombia	U	U	O	O	U	O
10.	Costa Rica	U	U	O	O	O	O
11.	Cyprus	U	U	U	O	O	O
14.	Egypt	O	O	O	U	U	U
15.	El Salvador	O	U	O	U	U	U
16.	Ethiopia	O	O	O	U	O	O
24.	Iran	O	O	O	O	O	I
25.	Iraq	U	O	U	O	U	U
28.	Jamaica	U	O	O	U	U	O
29.	Kenya	U	U	U	U	U	O
32.	Malaysia	U	U	O	O	U	U

Table IX.12. (continued)

SL. No.	Country	Structural equation			Reduced form equation		
		From total sample	From appropriate income group	From appropriate geographic region	From total sample	From appropriate income group	From appropriate geographic region
33.	Malta	U	O	U	O	O	U
35.	Morocco	O	O	O	U	U	U
37.	Pakistan	O	O	U	U	U	U
38.	Panama	O	U	O	O	O	O
39.	Paraguay	O	O	O	O	U	O
41.	Philippines	U	O	U	U	O	U
42.	Portugal	O	U	–	O	O	–
44.	Spain	U	U	–	O	O	–
45.	Sri Lanka	U	U	U	U	O	U
46.	Tanzania	U	U	U	O	O	O
49.	Turkey	O	U	O	O	O	U
52.	Japan	O	U	U	O	O	O

Note: Entry 'O' stands for 'Overachievers' and 'U' stands for 'Underachievers'.

CHAPTER X

CONCLUSIONS

The major aim of this study has been to examine empirically the role of foreign capital as a determinant of the behaviour of growth and savings in developing countries. In this chapter, we briefly summarize our methodological approach, major findings and their policy implications and suggest some directions for further research.

1. A BRIEF SUMMARY OF THE METHODOLOGY

The present study is essentially an international cross-section study. The study uses data on 52 developing countries for two time periods. The first time period covers 1950 to 1960 and the second period 1965 to 1973. This allows us to make comparisons between two historical time periods. Even though we have used data on both time periods separately, our emphasis has been more on the second period. Since aggregation bias may be very serious in aggregate cross-section data, we have followed two types of sample disaggregation while estimating our models. The first type of classification was based on three income groups to allow us to capture the impact of differences in the state of development of a country in a cross-section framework. The second type of classification was based on the geographic regions to capture the impact of differences in geographical, institutional and socio-cultural factors.

In the process of developing our analysis in the text, we have also estimated single equation models for savings and growth, inspite of our emphasis on the simultaneous equations approach. The major justifications for reporting single equation regressions are: (i) We have estimated these relations using more recent data; (ii) the specifications of our single equation relationships are more appropriate than those of previous studies in this area; (iii) these estimates allow us to compare our results with the single equation results of the previous studies; (iv) the simple models also allow us to compare the results with our own simultaneous equation results and finally, (v) we have been able to provide estimates based on far more disaggregated samples. In addition, following innovation by Papanek, we have decomposed the aggregate foreign capital into three parts, that is, foreign aid (*AID*), foreign private investment (*FPI*) and other capital inflows (*RFI*).

Given our reservations about single equation models, we have specified and estimated a simultaneous equations model in which both the savings rate and the growth rate are jointly determined. This procedure is more appropriate given our knowledge from the theoretical and empirical literature which suggests that savings and growth affect each other, that is, savings is a positive function of growth and at the same time growth is also a positive function of savings. Foreign capital appears as an explanatory variable in both equations although the direction in which foreign capital affects savings may be different than its effect on growth.

Using the simultaneous equations model, we have shown that foreign capital affects saving and growth both *directly*, as shown in the single equation models, but also indirectly, because of the interdependence between savings and growth. We have further shown that the *total effect*, which consists of both the *direct* and the *indirect* effects, may be different from the *direct* effect both in terms of the magnitude, and sometimes even more significant, in terms of the direction (that is the sign of the *total* and the *direct* effects may be opposite). Since the discussion in Chapter V is somewhat technical, here we provide a simpler discussion for the general reader.

To illustrate, let us consider the direct and total effects of foreign capital on domestic savings. We assume that foreign capital has a positive effect on growth and that growth has a positive effect on savings. Given these assumptions, three possible cases can be identified: (a) *Case 1*: direct effect of foreign capital on savings is negative and the total effect is also negative. But in this case, direct effect will overestimate the total effect because it cannot capture the indirect positive effects of foreign capital on saving via growth. This has been the case in usual single equation approaches in the previous studies. (b) *Case 2*: direct effect is negative but the total effect is positive; this is not impossible given that the indirect positive impact of foreign capital on savings via growth may be sufficiently large to generate such results. Thus, such results are not inconsistent, given the simultaneity in the relationships involved. (c) *Case 3*: direct effect of foreign capital on savings is positive and the total effect is also positive. But in this case, positive direct effect will underestimate the positive total effect, again for the same reason as above.

In a similar manner, we can identify three possible cases of the direct and total effect of foreign capital on growth. We assume that savings have a positive effect on growth. But foreign capital can have either negative or positive effect on savings. (a) *Case 1*: both direct and total effect of foreign capital on growth are positive and that direct effect of foreign capital on savings is negative. In this case, the positive direct effect will overestimate the positive total effect on growth. This is because the direct effect cannot discount the negative effect of foreign capital on growth via its negative direct effect on savings. (b) *Case 2*: direct effect is positive but total effect is negative. This can happen because of the same reason as in Case 1 except that the negative impact of foreign capital on growth via its negative impact on savings is sufficiently large to warrant such results. (c) *Case 3*: both direct and total effects are positive but the effect of foreign capital on savings is also positive. This will give us a result exactly opposite to that obtained in Case 1, that is, positive direct effect will underestimate the positive total effect of foreign capital on savings because the direct effect in this case cannot allow for the additional positive effect of foreign capital on growth via its positive impact on savings.

In estimating the simultaneous equations model, we have again followed the same procedure of sample disaggregation, variable disaggregation as well as estimating the relationships for both time periods as was done in the context of single equation models. This again allows us to make intertemporal as well as inter and intra-group comparisons vis-à-vis the aggregate results.

2. SUMMARY OF THE MAJOR FINDINGS AND SOME POLICY IMPLICATIONS

In this section, we summarize our main findings. To avoid repetition, the discussion is deliberately brief.

On the basis of our results from single and simultaneous equations models and on the basis of estimates from different level and type of sample disaggregation, we have found that the domestic savings as well as foreign capital make positive contribution to growth but that the former is relatively more important (in terms of magnitude as well as statistical significance of the coefficient estimates) than the latter. In the context of the single equation model, we have also observed that irrespective of the state of development in which a country operates, domestic savings retains its significaint positive contribution on growth, whereas it is not unambiguously true for foreign capital. This result is further confirmed by the regression results (both single and simultaneous equation results) on the basis of three income groups. This result suggests that while foreign capital is still useful, more effort should be given to mobilize resources from internal sources.

Given our observation that foreign capital has some positive role to play and that, whether one likes it or not, foreign capital will still continue to play a crucial role in the relations between the developed and the developing countries in the near future, we investigated the relative effectiveness of different types of foreign capital on domestic growth. In this exercise, we have examined the sensitivity of the coefficient estimates with respect to method of estimation (e.g., single equation versus simultaneous equation model), sample disaggregation into income and geographic groups as well as disaggregation of the aggregate foreign capital into three components.

Let us first consider the impact of foreign aid and foreign private investment only, withholding the discussion on other capital inflows until a later satge in this section. In examining the effect of foreign capital on growth, we will now refer to the three cases mentioned in Section 1. In terms of direct effects, both types of foreign capital have, in general, positive contribution and the direction of the total effect is parallel to the direction of the direct effect. In terms of the three cases, in most instances, the results fall in the category of Case 1 and in some instances Case 3. Since, in most instances, results fall in the category of Case 1, we conclude that the single equation models used in previous studies tend to overestimate the effect of foreign capital on growth because of these models' failure to capture the indirect negative effect of the relevant foreign capital on growth via this negative impact on domestic savings. This result holds for all three types of foreign capital.

Turning now to the ranking of the different types of foreign capital, the results of the single equation and the simultaneous equation models are not fully in agreement. Using single equation estimates, we have found that foreign aid is more productive than foreign private investment, and in most cases, the coefficient of foreign private investment is not significantly different from zero. This conclusion remained valid even when the marginal productivity of different types of foreign capital were allowed to vary depending on the state of development of a country. Further support in favour of this result was obtained from the regression results of the income and geographic groups. But the ranking is reversed when we considered the total effect derived from the reduced form coefficients. Here, we found in most cases that the positive total effect of foreign private investment was larger than that of foreign aid. This apparent inconsistency of results based on direct and total effect can be explained by our findings (explained later) that foreign aid has, in general, larger and more significant negative impact on domestic savings compared to foreign private investment. In any case, we cannot rely much on the ranking based on total effect mainly because the estimated structural coefficient of foreign private investment is not statistically significant. Thus, given our reliance on usual statistical criteria, and on the basis of strong evidence in favour of foreign aid against foreign private investment from single equation results, we are inclined to suggest that foreign aid is more useful than foreign private investment.

Let us now consider the relative effects of different types of foreign capital on domestic savings. The empirical results in this case are more ambiguous than those for growth. The results (in terms of sign, magnitude and statistical significance of the coefficient estimates) are much more sensitive to estimation methods as well as to the level and type of sample disaggregation. First, we consider the results of the single equation model. When foreign capital is used in the aggregate form, the sign of the coefficient is negative and statistically significant. This pattern holds even when the coefficients are estimated for disaggregated samples (income groups or geographic groups). For further analysis, when the aggregate foreign capital is decomposed into three component parts, the sign, the magnitude and the statistical significance of the estimated coefficients are affected. Further sensitivity of the results are obtained from sample disaggregation into income groups or geographic groups. Therefore, the sensitivity of these results indicate the extent of aggregation bias involved in using cross section data in aggregative form as well as using foreign capital in aggregate form. What is more interesting to note is the fact that the negative impact of foreign capital on domestic savings cannot be unambiguously stated.

We now return to the results of simultaneous equations model and the comparison of respective direct and indirect effects. In contrast to the results on growth, the results on savings are again much more ambiguous. As before, we will again refer to the three cases identified in Section 1 with regard to the impact on savings. In terms of the direct effects, no unambiguous sign pattern emerges. As a result, the sign of the total effect also does not follow any systematic pattern. Considering our results, we have found that all three cases are now possible although we have also found that the results in most instances tend to fall in the category of Case 1 followed by Case 2. Their implications are already described in Section 1. Since results in most instances fall in Case 1, we conclude that single equation results of the previous studies on savings tend to overestimate the adverse effect of foreign capital on domestic savings, keeping in mind that other cases are also possible. This is mainly because such models cannot take account of the positive indirect effect of the respective foreign capital on savings via its positive impact on growth.

With regard to the ranking, that is, the relative adverse effect of different types of foreign capital on domestic savings, the results of the single and simultaneous models are in agreement. This result is unlike the result we have obtained with respect to the impact on growth. From single equation results, we have found, in general, that foreign aid has greater adverse effect on savings than foreign private investment. This result holds in terms of the sign, the magnitude and the statistical significance of the coefficient estimates. More interesting to note is the result that in many cases, the negative coefficient of the foreign private investment is statistically insignificant and more surprisingly, in some cases, the sign is even positive (although not statistically significant always). The results based on total effects (from reduced form coefficients) support the ranking based on single equation results. These results sound plausible because foreign aid is negotiated on a government to governments basis and it is quite likely that the government of the recipient country may tend to relax its efforts to mobilize resources domestically once it has found large commitments of foreign aid from external sources.

We will now say a few words on other capital inflows. This type of capital inflow (*RFI*) does not provide an instrument of policy to the recipient country. It mostly consists of short-term capital flows and thus, is more determined by short-term economice forces rather than long-term considerations. In any case, allowing for the sensitivity of the results, we have, in general, found that other types of capital inflows have significant positive impact on growth as well as significant negative impact on savings. Like other results, this conclusion is also not very unambiguous and should be interpreted with caution.

In most of the cross-section studies, the conventional practice has been to pool countries over income groups, over geographical regions and even over different time periods. We have been able to show in many instances that such pooling and aggregation may lead to serious aggregation bias and sometimes, can give misleading results. This can happen because such aggregation may result in serious loss or even distortion of information inherent in the data. We have already found that the sign, magnitude and statistical significance of the coefficient estimates may change drastically when sample disaggregation is allowed. Thus, given a sample of aggregated cross-section data, if disaggregation is allowed, the researcher may be able to capture additional characteristics inherent in the data. For example, by disaggregating the sample into income groups, we were able to capture some of the effect of the differences in the state of development between different countries within the framework of cross-section studies. Similarly, sample disaggregation into geographic groups enabled us to delineate some differences in the characteristics with respect to geographic, socio-cultural and institutional aspects.

We have also found some additional justification of our sample disaggregation on the basis of stability analysis in Chapter VIII, between different time periods, over different income and geographic groups. In general, we have found that the savings function exhibited more structural instability than the growth function. In this study, we have further conducted some experiments to examine the relative performance of our estimated model in terms of within sample predictions (Chapter IX). Here again, in accordance with our a priori expectations, we have observed that the disaggregated results performed relatively bettern than those based on the aggregate sample, in deriving the predicted values closer to the actual values of the savings rate as well as the growth rate. We have found that, in this exercise, geographic grouping performed slightly better than grouping based on income, although this is by no means conclusive and should be treated with caution. In addition, we have examined the methodology of classifying countries as 'overachievers' and 'underachievers', as applied in some previous studies (see, for example, Papanek [43]). These classifications are done on the basis of comparing predicted values with actual values. The predicted values were usually derived from single equation regression models and using aggregate cross-country data. We have found that such results are very much sensitive to: (a) the form of equation used, i.e., whether structural or reduced form equation is used in deriving predicted values; and (b) the level and type of sample disaggregation i.e., whether predictions are derived from income groups or geographic groups.

Some of the policy implications of our major findings have already been alluded to. The most important one is that, although foreign capital has a positive role to play, capital accumulation from internal sources remains by far the most significant determinant of growth in developing countries. Consequently, if these countries wish to achieve rapid economic growth, maximum efforts will have to be directed towards raising domestic savings rates. This may involve difficult choices and necessitate tough and even unpleasant policies, but there is no escaping the implication that reliance on foreign capital does not offer the solution for high and rapid growth.

While developing countries will continue to be obliged to accept foreign capital, for example, in those areas where domestic resources do not provide an adequate substitute, the recipient country should be careful in deciding about the type of foreign investment it will encourage. The answer will depend on the relative productivity and effectiveness of different types of capital. We have previously suggested that other capital flows (*RFI*) do not provide a choice instrument, the real choice, if any, will remain between foreign aid and foreign private investment. The results of this study have suggested a slight advantage of foreign aid over foreign private investment, but this advantage is not very unambiguous. A careful interpretation of the results, in fact, will show that there is a tradeoff involved. The tradeoff arises because the two types of foreign capital influence savings and growth differently. For example, while foreign private investment has quantitatively less adverse effect on domestic savings compared to foreign aid, foreign aid makes a more significant contribution to growth relative to foreign private investment. Therefore, the real choice will depend on the demand and supply conditions encountered by a particular country. On the demand side, the choice will be influenced by the specific conditions and internal reaction patterns of economic forces within the domestic economy with respect to the two types of foreign capital. This will require an understanding of the mechanism through which different types of foreign capital flows influence the internal economic forces. A related question is, however, whether the recipient country has a choice in deciding the relative mix in which different types of foreign capital will be encouraged. The answer lies in the supply side conditions, i.e., it depends on the relative availability of the two types of foreign capital, the institutional set-up in which donor countries operate in the market for international capital and also the motivation of the donor countries. Given the relative bargaining power of the developing and the developed countries at the present time, it may well be the case that the recipient countries do not possess much freedom of choice.

3. SUGGESTIONS FOR FURTHER RESEARCH

Our study suggests a number of areas for further research. But the following three areas stand out to be the most important.

(i) We have tried to minimize some of the limitations inherent in aggregate cross-section studies by adopting the procedure of sample disaggregation. While such disaggregation is obviously useful and should be followed in future research dealing with cross-section data, it is clear that most useful insights can only be gained by individual country studies, and, therefore, future efforts should be devoted to such studies.

(ii) On the issue of the relative effectiveness of different types of foreign capital, the present study could not provide definitive answers. We have already indicated that, in such cases, a more detailed analysis to understand the mechanism through which different types of foreign capital influences internal economic forces will be much useful and illuminating. These types of studies are seriously lacking and such studies should be conducted at the level of individual or at least at the level of well defined groups of similar countries.

(iii) Along with sample disaggregation, we have found that the variable disaggregation also provides useful insights. While we have been able to disaggregate foreign capital into three components, we have used certain other variables such as growth of GNP and savings rate in highly aggregated form. For example, domestic savings could as well be decomposed into urban versus rural savings and private versus public savings. It would be interesting to examine whether and to what extent different types of foreign capital have differential impact on different types of domestic savings. One obvious hypothesis that emerges from this study is to test whether foreign aid and foreign private investment affect private and public domestic savings differently. Such disaggregations may provide useful and illuminating results for policy purposes.

APPENDIX A

THE SAMPLE

A. THE COMPOSITION OF THE AGGREGATE SAMPLE

The initial cross-section sample with which Gupta [30] worked consisted of 40 developing countries for 1960s. The present study is mainly based on an extended sample of 52 developing countries including those initial 40 countries. The relevant data for the 52 countries were collected separately for two time periods i.e. 1950s and 1970s in order to enable us to make some intertemporal comparisons. The first one covers the time period 1950 to 1960 and the second one covers the period 1965 to 1973. The countries are derived mainly from three geographic regions i.e. Asia, Africa and Southern Europe, and Latin America. The 52 countries are listed below:

1. Afghanistan; 2. Algeria; 3. Argentina; 4. Bolivia; 5. Brazil; 6. Burma; 7. Chad; 8. Chile; 9. Colombia; 10. Costa Rica; 11. Cyprus; 12. Dominican Republic; 13. Ecuador; 14. Egypt; 15. El Salvador; 16. Ethiopia; 17. Ghana; 18. Greece; 19. Guatemala; 20. Guyana; 21. Honduras; 22. India; 23. Indonesia; 24. Iran; 25. Iraq; 26. Israel; 27. Ivory Coast; 28. Jamaica; 29. Kenya; 30. Korea (Republic); 31. Lebanon; 32. Malaysia; 33. Malta; 34. Mexico; 35. Morocco; 36. Nicaragua; 37. Pakistan; 38. Panama; 39. Paraguay; 40. Peru; 41. Philippines; 42. Portugal; 43. Saudi Arabia; 44. Spain; 45. Sri Lanka; 46. Tanzania; 47. Thailand; 48. Trinidad-Tobago; 49. Turkey; 50. Uruguay; 51. Venezuela; 52. Japan.

B. SAMPLE DISAGGREGATION INTO INCOME GROUPS

The purpose of disaggregation into income groups is discussed in the text. The sample of 52 countries has been disaggregated into three major income groups on the basis of 1973 per capita income. Group I comprises those countries whose per capita income is less than US $300; similarily, group II involves countries within the income range of $301 and $600 and that of group III as having per capita income greater than $600. The classification of the countries as above are given below:

Group I ($y < \$300$)	Group II ($\$300 < y < \$600$)	Group III ($y > \$600$)
1. Afghanistan	2. Algeria	3. Argentina
4. Bolivia	5. Brazil	8. Chile
6. Burma	9. Colombia	10. Costa Rica
7. Chad	12. Dom. Republic	11. Cyprus
14. Egypt	13. Ecuador	18. Greece
16. Ethiopia	15. El Salvador	24. Iran
17. Ghana	19. Guatemala	25. Iraq
22. India	20. Guyana	26. Israel
23. Indonesia	21. Honduras	28. Jamaica
29. Kenya	27. Ivory Coast	31. Lebanon
37. Pakistan	30. Korea (R.)	33. Malta
41. Philippines	32. Malaysia	34. Mexico
45. Sri Lanka	35. Morocco	38. Panama
46. Tanzania	36. Nicaragua	40. Peru
47. Thailand	39. Paraguay	42. Portugal
	49. Turkey	43. Saudi Arabia
		44. Spain
		48. Trinidad-Tobago
		50. Uruguay
		51. Venezuela
		52. Japan

C. SAMPLE DISAGGREGATION INTO GEOGRAPHIC REGIONS

The 52 countries are classified into three major geographic regions as follows:

Asia	Africa & Southern Europe	Latin America
1. Afghanistan	2. Algeria	3. Argentina
6. Burma	7. Chad	4. Bolivia
11. Cyprus	14. Egypt	5. Brazil
22. India	16. Ethiopia	8. Chile
23. Indonesia	17. Ghana	9. Colombia
24. Iran	18. Greece	10. Costa Rica
25. Iraq	27. Ivory Coast	12. Dom. Republic
26. Israel	29. Kenya	13. Ecuador
30. Korea (R.)	33. Malta	15. El Salvador

Asia	Africa & Southern Europe	Latin America
31. Lebanon	35. Morocco	19. Guatemala
32. Malaysia	42. Portugal	20. Guyana
37. Pakistan	44. Spain	21. Honduras
41. Philippines	46. Tanzania	28. Jamaica
43. Saudi Arabia		34. Mexico
45. Sri Lanka		36. Nicaragua
47. Thailand		38. Panama
49. Turkey		39. Paraguay
52. Japan		40. Peru
		48. Trinidad-Tobago
		50. Uruguay
		51. Venezuela

APPENDIX B

THE SOURCES OF DATA AND THE DEFINITION OF THE VARIABLES USED

A. THE SOURCES OF DATA

Various economic and demographic variables were used in this study. The major source of data for almost all of the variables used in this study has been the *World Tables* published by the World Bank, John Hopkins Press, Baltimore, U.S.A. The data for the 1950s were mainly taken from the World Tables 1971 and for the time period 1965–1973 were taken from World Tables 1976. Minor supplements to the data were made from various issues of the UN Yearbook of National Accounts Statistics and in some cases, the International Financial Statistics of the International Monetary Fund (IMF).

B. THE DEFINITION AND MEASUREMENT OF VARIABLES

(1) *Gross National Product* (Y): GNP at constant factor cost is the value of Gross National Product excluding indirect taxes net of subsidies.

(2) *Growth Rate of GNP* (G *or* $\Delta Y/Y$): This variable is measured as the annual average compound rate of growth of GNP over the relevant time period, i.e. 1950–1960 for the first period and 1965–1973 for the second period. The growth rate data are available in World Tables 1971 and World Tables 1976, respectively for the two periods.

(3) *Per Capita GNP* (y *or* Y/P): GNP per capita is derived simply by dividing GNP in US dollars by the size of the midyear population.

(4) *Population* (P): Population figures for each country are midyear estimates (July 1) by the UN statistical office or the World Bank.

(5) *Labour Force* (L): It indicates economically active labour force, including armed forces and unemployed but excluding housewives, students and other inactive groups. The relevant data on L for each country in the sample for 1960 and 1970 are available in the World Tables 1976.

(6) *Growth of the Labour Force* (GL *or* $\Delta L/L$): Growth rate of the labour force is calculated as annual average growth rate of the economically active labour force (L) over the period 1960 and 1970.

(7) *Savings Ratio* (S/Y): It is measured as gross domestic savings expressed as percentage of the GNP at current market prices and local currencies for

individual countries. Gross domestic savings is measured as gross domestic investment at current prices plus exports of goods and non-factor services less import of goods and non-factor services.

(8) *Ratio of Aggregate Foreign Capital Inflow* (F/Y): This is measured as the deficit/surplus in the current account (excluding unrequited transfers to and from abroad) as a percentage of GNP.

(9) *Ratio of Foreign Aid to GNP* (*AID or* F_1/Y): Foreign aid is a major component of aggregate foreign capital inflow. This is measured as net transfers received by governments plus official long-term borrowing expressed as a percentage of GNP. This includes net value of loans extended by non-residents for periods extending over one year to the public sector or to the private sector under a public sector guarantee for repayment.

(10) *Ratio of Foreign Private Investment* (*FPI or* F_2/Y): Foreign private investment includes private long-term borrowing plus net private direct investment. These are expressed as a percentage of GNP.

(11) *Ratio of Other Capital Inflows to GNP* (*RFI or* F_3/Y): This indicates net private transfers, net short-term borrowing, other capital (net), and errors and omissions in the balance of payments as percentage of GNP.

(12) *Energy Consumption Per Worker* (*EN*): It refers to the apparent annual inland consumption per capita of all types of commercial fuels – coal, coke, lignite, petroleum, and petroleum products, natural and manufactured gas, electricity and peat – converted into kilograms of coal equivalents. This variable is used as a proxy to measure other variables such as the capital stock (K) or the state of development of an economy (*SD*).

(13) *Percentage of Labour Force in Agriculture* (*ALF*): It indicates agricultural labour force as a percentage of the total labour force. Agricultural activities include farming, forestry, hunting, and fishing.

(14) *State of Development* (*SD*): There is no direct measure for this variable. Variables such as GNP per capita, energy consumption per capita, or percentage of labour force in agriculture (these are defined above) are used to measure the state of development of a country.

(15) *Dependency Rate* (*DR*): It is measured as the population under 15 and over 65 years of age, divided by the labour force in the age group 15–65 years.

(16) *Number of Persons per Hospital Bed* (*HB*): It is defined as the population divided by the number of hospital beds available in public and private general and specialized hospitals, medical centres, bedded dispensaries, leprosaria, etc.

(17) *Literacy Rate* (*ED*): it is used as an index of education and is

measured by the number of literate adults as a percentage of the total adult population 15 years of age and over. Literacy is defined as the ability both to read and to write.

(18) *Population Density* (*DEN*): This density refers to total land area of a country and is measured by midyear population per square kilometer (100 hectares) of total land.

(19) *Birth Rate* (*BR*): It refers to crude birth rate which indicates annual live births per thousand of midyear population.

(20) *Infant Mortality Rate* (*IMR*): It indicates annual deaths under one year of age per thousand live births.

(21) *Capital Stock* (*K*): It is measured by energy consumption per capita (*EN*) which is already defined above.

(22) *Female Participation Rate* (*FPR*): It indicates the percentage of women in the labour force and is measured by the number of female labour force as a percentage of the total labour force.

(23) *Total Labour Force Participation Rate* (*TLPR*): It is measured by the number of active labour force as a percentage of the midyear population for each country.

APPENDIX C

THE REDUCED FORM EQUATIONS AND ELASTICITY MULTIPLIER TABLES

TABLE C1
Reduced form of the nine simultaneous equation model of growth (1970s): OLS estimates ($n = 52$)

Endogenous variables	Exogenous Variables								
	Constant	*AID*	*FPI*	*RFI*	*EN*	*DEN*	*LIT*	*GL*	*HB*
S/Y	0.1252	−0.4681	0.0069	−1.1204	0.00	0.00	0.0331	0.0714	0.00
G	0.0288	0.1776	0.1622	0.1486	0.00	0.00	0.0087	0.0585	0.00
y	−15.3519	0.00	0.00	0.00	0.5217	−0.0162	6.1209	0.00	−0.0005
TLPR	0.3008	0.00	0.00	0.00	0.00	0.00	0.0604	0.00	0.00
DR	1.7180	0.00	0.00	0.00	−0.0001	0.00	−0.3620	0.00	0.00
BR	52.0520	0.00	0.00	0.00	−0.0028	0.0001	−1.9154	0.00	0.0002
FPR	22.8546	0.00	0.00	0.00	−0.0012	0.00	5.6932	0.00	−0.0001
IMR	122.2436	0.00	0.00	0.00	−0.0086	0.0003	−1.0890	0.00	0.0097
ALF	64.0469	0.00	0.00	0.00	−0.0104	0.0003	−1.2436	0.00	0.00

TABLE C2
Reduced form of the nine simultaneous equation model of growth (1970s) for income group I: OLS estimates ($n = 15$)

Endogenous variables	Exogenous Variables								
	Constant	*AID*	*FPI*	*RFI*	*EN*	*DEN*	*LIT*	*GL*	*HB*
S/Y	0.0657	0.6942	1.3078	0.9048	0.0002	–0.0001	0.0102	0.0325	0.00
G	0.0166	0.5691	0.8081	0.4089	0.0001	0.00	0.0025	0.0178	0.00
y	61.6900	0.00	0.00	0.00	0.8643	–0.5040	2.2547	0.00	0.00
TLPR	0.3782	0.00	0.00	0.00	0.00	0.00	0.0059	0.00	0.00
DR	1.3486	0.00	0.00	0.00	0.00	0.00	–0.0210	0.00	0.00
BR	50.5223	0.00	0.00	0.00	–0.0044	0.0026	–1.6645	0.00	0.001
FPR	29.9368	0.00	0.00	0.00	–0.0228	0.0133	3.0540	0.00	0.00
IMR	150.6981	0.00	0.00	0.00	–0.0651	0.0380	–1.6978	0.00	0.00
ALF	77.7047	0.00	0.00	0.00	–0.0651	0.0380	–1.6978	0.00	0.00

TABLE C3
Reduced form of the nine simultaneous equation model of growth for income group II: OLS estimates (n = 16)

Endogenous variables	Exogenous Variables								
	Constant	*AID*	*FPI*	*RFI*	*EN*	*DEN*	*LIT*	*GL*	*HB*
S/Y	0.1017	1.5390	−0.2148	−1.3368	0.00	−0.0001	0.0455	0.0283	0.00
G	0.0345	0.2435	−0.2073	0.2590	0.00	0.00	0.0125	0.0585	0.00
y	359.7051	0.00	0.00	0.00	0.1160	−0.5894	1.6691	0.00	0.00
TLPR	0.2601	0.00	0.00	0.00	0.00	0.00	0.0891	0.00	0.00
DR	1.9895	0.00	0.00	0.00	0.00	0.0001	−0.4999	0.00	0.00
BR	53.2805	0.00	0.00	0.00	−0.0007	0.0037	−1.9831	0.00	0.00
FPR	19.1995	0.00	0.00	0.00	0.00	0.0001	1.1677	0.00	0.00
IMR	96.4059	0.00	0.00	0.00	0.0088	−0.0449	−3.8226	0.00	0.00
ALF	54.2055	0.00	0.00	0.00	−0.0014	0.0070	−1.9696	0.00	0.00

TABLE C4

Reduced form of the nine simultaneous equation model of growth for income group III: OLS estimates ($n = 21$)

Endogenous variables	Exogenous Variables								
	Constant	*AID*	*FPI*	*RFI*	*EN*	*DEN*	*LIT*	*GL*	*HB*
S/Y	0.2220	2.2163	0.1761	1.7722	0.00	0.00	0.0300	0.0240	0.000
G	0.0529	0.2144	0.1709	0.0233	0.00	0.00	–0.0105	0.0241	0.000
y	898.0331	0.00	0.00	0.00	0.3501	0.0060	1.9789	0.00	–0.1606
TLPR	0.2599	0.00	0.00	0.00	0.00	0.00	0.1094	0.00	0.000
DR	1.9246	0.00	0.00	0.00	0.00	0.00	–0.7459	0.00	0.0002
BR	53.6026	0.00	0.00	0.00	–0.0015	0.00	–2.9364	0.00	0.0067
FPR	16.5789	0.00	0.00	0.00	0.0008	0.00	8.1056	0.00	–0.0020
IMR	134.4194	0.00	0.00	0.00	–0.0034	–0.0001	–1.1152	0.00	0.0355
ALF	34.0532	0.00	0.00	0.00	–0.0023	0.00	–0.1326	0.00	0.0011

TABLE C5
Reduced form of the nine simultaneous equation model of growth for Asia: OLS estimates ($n = 18$)

Endogenous variables	Exogenous Variables								
	Constant	*AID*	*FPI*	*RFI*	*EN*	*DEN*	*LIT*	*GL*	*HB*
S/Y	0.0632	−2.0051	1.2066	−0.1299	0.00	0.00	0.0953	0.3438	0.00
G	−0.0135	0.3306	1.0236	−0.0581	0.00	0.00	0.0334	0.1937	0.00
y	159.6622	0.00	0.00	0.00	1.2400	−1.3383	−1.2477	0.00	0.0009
TLPR	0.2741	0.00	0.00	0.00	0.00	0.00	0.1161	0.00	0.00
DR	1.6829	0.00	0.00	0.00	−0.0001	0.0001	−0.5329	0.00	0.00
BR	55.8278	0.00	0.00	0.00	−0.0026	0.0028	−2.6780	0.00	0.0003
FPR	12.7106	0.00	0.00	0.00	−0.0038	0.0042	2.8239	0.00	−0.0003
IMR	158.8256	0.00	0.00	0.00	−0.0168	0.0181	−1.0767	0.00	0.0047
ALF	61.4570	0.00	0.00	0.00	−0.0184	0.0198	1.8466	0.00	0.00

TABLE C6
Reduced form of the nine simultaneous equation model of growth (1970s) for Africa: OLS estimates ($n = 10$)

Endogenous variables	Exogenous Variables								
	Constant	*AID*	*FPI*	*RFI*	*EN*	*DEN*	*LIT*	*GL*	*HB*
S/Y	−0.0168	−0.3606	−6.6967	1.2605	0.0006	0.00	−0.0660	0.5228	0.00
G	−0.0111	0.0285	−1.9968	0.1601	0.0002	0.00	−0.0201	0.1843	0.00
y	71.5931	0.00	0.00	0.00	1.2529	−0.0299	−1.7070	0.00	0.00
TLPR	0.3318	0.00	0.00	0.00	0.00	0.00	0.1069	0.00	0.00
DR	1.6697	0.00	0.00	0.00	−0.0001	0.00	−0.5162	0.00	0.00
BR	55.8674	0.00	0.00	0.00	−0.0048	0.0001	−3.8523	0.00	0.00
FPR	34.6941	0.00	0.00	0.00	−0.0136	0.0003	−5.3444	0.00	0.00
IMR	145.3716	0.00	0.00	0.00	−0.0514	0.0012	−8.8237	0.00	0.0002
ALF	87.3490	0.00	0.00	0.00	−0.1054	0.0025	1.4356	0.00	0.00

TABLE C7
Reduced form of the nine equation model of growth for Latin America: OLS estimates ($n = 21$)

Endogenous variables	Exogenous Variables								
	Constant	*AID*	*FPI*	*RFI*	*EN*	*DEN*	*LIT*	*GL*	*HB*
S/Y	0.0854	0.3280	0.0840	−0.3583	0.00	−0.0001	0.0706	0.0168	0.00
G	0.0295	0.1435	0.1327	0.2690	0.00	0.00	0.0021	0.0580	0.00
y	−85.2034	0.00	0.00	0.00	0.2022	−1.6711	9.7338	0.00	−0.0008
TLPR	0.2814	0.00	0.00	0.00	0.00	−0.0001	0.0563	0.00	0.00
DR	1.9082	0.00	0.00	0.00	−0.0001	0.0004	−0.4003	0.00	0.00
BR	51.4155	0.00	0.00	0.00	−0.0022	0.0183	−1.7035	0.00	0.0002
FPR	18.5596	0.00	0.00	0.00	0.0011	−0.0093	5.2235	0.00	0.00
IMR	89.2369	0.00	0.00	0.00	−0.0061	0.0507	−2.6893	0.00	−0.0059
ALF	66.1028	0.00	0.00	0.00	−0.0062	0.0516	−3.0077	0.00	0.00

TABLE C8
Elasticity multipliers of the nine simultaneous equation model of growth (1970s): OLS estimates ($n = 52$)

Endogenous variables	Exogenous variables							
	AID	*FPI*	*RFI*	*EN*	*DEN*	*LIT*	*GL*	*HB*
S/Y	−0.0598	0.0005	−0.0757	0.1163	−0.0004	0.1387	0.1108	−0.0003
G	0.0614	0.0346	0.022	0.0823	−0.0003	0.0982	0.2235	−0.0002
y	0.00	0.00	0.00	0.5477	−0.0019	0.5160	0.00	−0.0003
TLPR	0.00	0.00	0.00	0.0217	−0.0001	0.1185	0.00	−0.0007
DR	0.00	0.00	0.00	−0.0311	0.0001	−0.1700	0.00	0.0010
BR	0.00	0.00	0.00	−0.0663	0.0002	−0.3630	0.00	0.0022
FPR	0.00	0.00	0.00	−0.0407	0.0001	0.1511	0.00	−0.0013
IMR	0.00	0.00	0.00	−0.1083	0.0004	−0.1082	0.00	0.0740
ALF	0.00	0.00	0.00	−0.2023	0.0007	−0.1906	0.00	0.0001

TABLE C9
Elasticity multipliers of the nine simultaneous equation model of growth for income group I: OLS estimates ($n = 15$)

Endogenous variables	Exogenous variables							
	AID	*FPI*	*RFI*	*EN*	*DEN*	*LIT*	*GL*	*HB*
S/Y	0.0887	0.1030	0.0611	1.2583	–0.0829	0.0426	0.0459	–0.0001
G	0.1967	0.1709	0.0748	0.8422	–0.0555	0.0285	0.0682	–0.0001
y	0.00	0.00	0.00	0.9074	–0.0598	0.0187	0.00	0.00
TLPR	0.00	0.00	0.00	0.0039	–0.0003	0.0116	0.00	–0.0001
DR	0.00	0.00	0.00	–0.0033	0.0022	–0.0098	0.00	0.0001
BR	0.00	0.00	0.00	–0.1051	0.0069	–0.3155	0.00	0.0018
FPR	0.00	0.00	0.00	–0.7674	0.0505	0.0810	0.00	–0.0006
IMR	0.00	0.00	0.00	–1.5760	0.1038	–0.7011	0.00	0.0412
ALF	0.00	0.00	0.00	–1.2622	0.0831	–0.0260	0.00	0.00

TABLE C10

Elasticity multipliers of the nine simultaneous equation model of growth for income group II: OLS estimates ($n = 16$)

Endogenous variables	Exogenous variables							
	AID	*FPI*	*RFI*	*EN*	*DEN*	*LIT*	*GL*	*HB*
S/Y	0.1965	−0.0169	−0.0903	0.0767	−0.0440	0.1907	0.0399	0.00
G	0.0842	−0.0442	0.0474	0.0570	−0.0327	0.1418	0.2234	0.00
y	0.00	0.00	0.00	0.1218	−0.0699	0.1384	0.00	0.00
TLPR	0.00	0.00	0.00	0.0081	−0.0046	0.1747	0.00	0.00
DR	0.00	0.00	0.00	−0.0108	0.0062	−0.2347	0.00	0.00
BR	0.00	0.00	0.00	−0.0173	0.0099	−0.3759	0.00	0.00
FPR	0.00	0.00	0.00	−0.0010	0.0006	0.3099	0.00	0.00
IMR	0.00	0.00	0.00	0.1112	−0.0638	−0.3798	0.00	−0.0011
ALF	0.00	0.00	0.00	−0.0265	0.0152	−0.0302	0.00	0.00

TABLE C11
Elasticity multipliers of the nine simultaneous equation model of growth for income group III: OLS estimates (n = 21)

Endogenous variables	Exogenous variables							
	AID	*FPI*	*RFI*	*EN*	*DEN*	*LIT*	*GL*	*HB*
S/Y	−0.2830	0.0139	−0.1198	0.1182	0.0002	−0.1257	0.0339	−0.0121
G	0.0741	0.0364	0.0043	0.1121	0.0002	−0.1193	0.0925	−0.0115
y	0.00	0.00	0.00	0.3676	0.0007	0.0164	0.00	−0.1021
TLPR	0.00	0.00	0.00	0.0136	0.00	0.2146	0.00	−0.0377
DR	0.00	0.00	0.00	−0.0222	0.00	−0.3502	0.00	0.0615
BR	0.00	0.00	0.00	−0.0352	−0.0001	−0.5565	0.00	0.0977
FPR	0.00	0.00	0.00	0.0264	0.0001	0.2151	0.00	−0.0413
IMR	0.00	0.00	0.00	−0.0429	−0.0001	−1.1082	0.00	0.2702
ALF	0.00	0.00	0.00	−0.0455	−0.0001	−0.0020	0.00	0.0126

TABLE C12

Elasticity multipliers of the nine simultaneous equation model of growth (1970s) for Asia: OLS estimates ($n = 18$)

Endogenous variables	Exogenous variables							
	AID	*FPI*	*RFI*	*EN*	*DEN*	*LIT*	*GL*	*HB*
S/Y	0.2561	0.0950	−0.1299	0.0888	−0.0108	0.3993	0.4853	−0.0030
G	0.1143	0.2181	−0.0581	0.0843	−0.0103	0.3790	0.7399	−0.0028
y	0.00	0.00	0.00	1.3018	−0.1587	−0.1035	0.00	0.0006
TLPR	0.00	0.00	0.00	0.0276	−0.0034	0.2276	0.00	−0.0017
DR	0.00	0.00	0.00	−0.0303	0.0037	−0.2503	0.00	0.0019
BR	0.00	0.00	0.00	−0.0614	0.0075	−0.5075	0.00	0.0038
FPR	0.00	0.00	0.00	−0.1292	0.0157	0.7494	0.00	−0.0056
IMR	0.00	0.00	0.00	−0.2112	0.0257	−1.0690	0.00	0.0357
ALF	0.00	0.00	0.00	−0.3559	0.0434	0.0283	0.00	−0.0002

TABLE C13
Elasticity multipliers of the nine simultaneous equation model of growth for Africa: OLS estimates ($n = 10$)

Endogenous variables	Exogenous variables							
	AID	*FPI*	*RFI*	*EN*	*DEN*	*LIT*	*GL*	*HB*
S/Y	–0.0461	–0.5273	–0.0852	3.1934	–0.0086	–0.2767	0.7380	0.00
G	0.0099	–0.4255	0.0293	2.6265	–0.0071	–0.2276	0.7040	0.00
y	0.00	0.00	0.00	1.3153	–0.0035	–0.1416	0.00	0.00
TLPR	0.00	0.00	0.00	0.0327	–0.0001	0.2097	0.00	0.0001
DR	0.00	0.00	0.00	–0.0378	0.0001	–0.2424	0.00	–0.0001
BR	0.00	0.00	0.00	–0.1140	0.0003	–0.7301	0.00	–0.0002
FPR	0.00	0.00	0.00	–0.4554	0.0012	–0.1418	0.00	–0.0001
IMR	0.00	0.00	0.00	–0.6464	0.0017	–0.8768	0.00	0.0015
ALF	0.00	0.00	0.00	–2.0435	0.0055	0.2200	0.00	0.00

TABLE C14

Elasticity multipliers of the nine simultaneous equation model of growth on Latin America: OLS estimates ($n = 21$)

Endogenous variables	Exogenous variables							
	AID	*FPI*	*RFI*	*EN*	*DEN*	*LIT*	*GL*	*HB*
S/Y	0.0419	0.0066	–0.0242	0.0799	–0.0746	0.2961	0.0237	0.00
G	0.0496	0.0283	0.0492	0.0064	–0.0060	0.0238	0.2216	0.00
y	0.00	0.00	0.00	0.2123	–0.1981	0.8074	0.00	–0.0005
TLPR	0.00	0.00	0.00	0.0182	–0.0169	0.1105	0.00	–0.0011
DR	0.00	0.00	0.00	–0.0309	0.0288	–0.1880	0.00	0.0018
BR	0.00	0.00	0.00	–0.0531	0.0495	–0.3228	0.00	0.0031
FPR	0.00	0.00	0.00	0.0379	–0.0354	0.1386	0.00	0.0001
IMR	0.00	0.00	0.00	–0.0772	0.0720	–0.2672	0.00	–0.0448
ALF	0.00	0.00	0.00	–0.1212	0.1131	–0.4609	0.00	0.0003

TABLE C15
Reduced form of the seven simultaneous equation model of growth (1960s): 2SLS estimates[a] (n = 40)

Endogenous variables	Exogenous variables							
	AID	*FPI*	*RFI*	*EN*	*DEN*	*LIT*	*ALF*	*HB*
S/Y	−0.4872	−1.2455	−0.3688	0.0035	−0.0013	0.0089	−0.1540	0.00
G	0.1146	0.0905	0.2669	0.0003	−0.0001	0.0007	−0.0129	0.00
DR	0.00	0.00	0.00	0.0009	−0.0004	0.0482	0.2718	−0.00
BR	0.00	0.00	0.00	0.0017	−0.0006	0.0877	0.4944	−0.00
y	0.00	0.00	0.00	0.1963	−0.0749	1.2655	−3.4305	0.00
FPR	0.00	0.00	0.00	−0.0014	0.0005	−0.0715	−0.0956	0.00
IMR	0.00	0.00	0.00	−0.0005	0.0002	−0.3994	0.9110	−0.00003

[a] *Source*: Gupta [33].

TABLE C16
Reduced form of the seven simultaneous equation model of growth (1970s): 2SLS estimates ($n = 40$)

Endogenous variables	Exogenous variables								
	Constant	*AID*	*FPI*	*RFI*	*EN*	*DEN*	*LIT*	*ALF*	*HB*
S/Y	0.1490	−0.5149	0.0150	−1.0560	0.00	0.00	0.0436	−0.0002	0.00
G	0.0447	0.1324	0.1563	0.2506	0.00	0.00	0.0097	−0.0001	0.00
DR	1.5130	0.00	0.00	0.00	0.00	0.00	−0.2605	0.0030	0.00
BR	39.8557	0.00	0.00	0.00	0.0017	−0.0006	−1.5786	0.1828	0.00
y	−171.2184	0.00	0.00	0.00	0.5027	0.1788	−7.4366	0.8143	0.00
FPR	12.0857	0.00	0.00	0.00	0.0009	0.0003	8.2846	0.1578	0.00
IMR	101.8736	0.00	0.00	0.00	−0.0081	−0.0029	−6.7527	0.3447	0.0073

TABLE C17
Elasticity multipliers of the seven simultaneous equation model of growth (1960s): 2SLS estimates[a] ($n = 40$)

Endogenous variables	Exogenous variables							
	AID	*FPI*	*RFI*	*EN*	*DEN*	*LIT*	*ALF*	*HB*
S/Y	–0.1080	–0.1289	0.0027	0.1626	–0.0092	0.0376	–0.5252	0.0006
G	0.0657	0.0242	–0.0050	0.0353	–0.0020	0.0082	–0.1140	0.0001
DR	0.00	0.00	0.00	0.0150	–0.0009	0.0712	0.3252	–0.0004
BR	0.00	0.00	0.00	0.0294	–0.0017	0.1399	0.6392	–0.0008
y	0.00	0.00	0.00	0.3895	–0.0221	0.2275	–0.4996	0.0006
FPR	0.00	0.00	0.00	–0.0516	0.0029	–0.2456	–0.2661	0.0013
IMR	0.00	0.00	0.00	–0.0042	0.0002	–0.3192	0.5899	–0.0027

a *Source*: Gupta [30].

TABLE C18
Elasticity multipliers of the seven simultaneous equation model of growth (1970s): 2SLS estimates ($n = 40$)

Endogenous variables	Exogenous variables							
	AID	*FPI*	*RFI*	*EN*	*DEN*	*LIT*	*ALF*	*HB*
S/Y	−0.0658	0.0012	−0.0714	0.0893	0.0036	0.1829	−0.0644	0.00
G	0.0458	0.0333	0.0468	0.0535	0.0021	0.1095	−0.0386	0.00
DR	0.00	0.00	0.00	−0.0169	−0.0007	−0.1223	0.0924	0.00
BR	0.00	0.00	0.00	−0.0413	−0.0017	−0.2992	0.2261	0.00
y	0.00	0.00	0.00	0.5278	0.0212	0.6168	0.0441	0.00
FPR	0.00	0.00	0.00	0.0304	0.0012	0.2199	0.2733	0.00
IMR	0.00	0.00	0.00	−0.1018	−0.0041	−0.6710	0.2235	0.0556

NOTES

CHAPTER I

1 Relevant studies are surveyed in Chapter III and IV.

CHAPTER II

1 For a detailed discussion of the growth and importance of multinational corporations, see M. P. Todaro [61], pp. 400–402.
2 For the definition and classification of aggregate foreign capital into three components, see Appendix B.
3 The basis of classification into income and geographic groups and the composition of different sample groups has been discussed in Appendix A.
4 It is well known that aggregation bias can often lead to misleading results. See, for example, Gupta [29, 30].

CHAPTER III

1 See also Wasow [65].
2 See also Gulati [28] and Ram [50].
3 Papanek also tried education, population and per capita income, but without any success.
4 This point was recognized by Stoneman, though he did not offer any solution for it.
5 See, for example, Gupta [29, 30].
6 Details of the data are given in Appendix A.
7 We also experimented with some other variables as a proxy. These were: (a) energy consumption per worker; (b) ratio of non-agricultural to total labor force. However, these proxies did not perform any better.
8 Even using two state of development variables created severe multicollinearity problems.
9 The results in these columns improve dramatically which clearly highlights the problem created by multicollinearity.
10 Similar result was reported by Papanek [48]. However, Robinson [52] reported opposite result for this variable.
11 The relevant productivity coefficients are calculated as follows: As an example, let us take the case of foreign aid (*AID*). Its productivity

$$MPP_{F_1} = [\hat{\alpha}_4 + \hat{\alpha}_5(y)] = 0.13 + 0.0003(y).$$

The relevant $\hat{\alpha}i$'s are taken from Table III.2.

[12] This procedure also captures the non-linearity noticed by Stoneman [58]. But Stoneman did nothing to check whether his results were sensitive to the existence of non-linearities in the effects of inflows on growth.

CHAPTER IV

[1] There are some differences between the model used by Papanek and the one used in column (2) of Table IV.2. However, it is doubtful whether the differences can be attributed to this difference in specification. This can be seen by looking at columns (3) and (4) of Table IV.2.

CHAPTER V

[1] We only concentrate on Bacha's first model in which growth is constrained by savings.
[2] This critique is based on Gupta [34].
[3] This section draws upon Gupta [33].
[4] See, for example, Gregory *et al.* [22].

CHAPTER VI

[1] These variables are called endogenous because their values are determined within the system. The variables which are not determined within the system are usually called predetermined variables or exogenous variables. For detailed analysis see Goldberger [20].
[2] For the use of such a proxy, see Kim [38].
[3] See also Enke [16] on how increasing fertility by changing the dependency rate lowers per capita income. For the use of a similar equation, see Gregory *et al., op. cit.*
[4] See also Gregory *et al., op. cit.*, for the use of such a relationship.
[5] Leff *op. cit.*, page 887.
[6] Schultz, *op. cit.*, p. 155. See also Mincer, *op. cit.*, and Cain, *op. cit.*
[7] Schultz, *op. cit.*
[8] Schultz, *op. cit.*
[9] Becker [4].
[10] Benham [5], Cain, *op. cit.*

CHAPTER VII

[1] A. S. Goldberger [20]. In order tc calculate these multipliers, we must assume that $\hat{A}^{-1}$ exists.
[2] However, since OLS gave better results, the 2SLS reduced forms are not reported.
[3] It should be noted that the reduced form tables do not show the impact of per capita income, the growth rate, and the dependency rate on the saving and growth rate. This is because all of these variables are endogenous. However, their impact can be calculated

by following the methodology proposed by Gregory *et al.* [22]. It involves calculating *intercept* multipliers. The intercept elasticity is measured using the reduced form. It measures the percentage change in, say, the saving rate caused by a given percentage increase in the intercept of the income function. However, although these intercept multipliers were calculated, they are not being reported here because the information provided by them is not of primary concern for this study.

CHAPTER VIII

1 In a strict sense, one should not apply the Chow test when the relationships are simultaneous. To apply this test, the explanatory variables should be strictly exogenous, which is not true in the case of our model. But since tests have not been developed to deal with this type of problem, we still apply it even though it is not exactly appropriate.
2 G. S. Maddala ([42], p. 198). Maddala pointed out that the test which econometricians call the Chow test was in fact derived much earlier by C. R. Rao and others. See C. R. Rao [51]. Maddala suggests not to attach any name to the test.
3 The respective degrees of freedom in the three group case are calculated as follows:
(i) e_p^2 is ss. residuals from pooled sample with $(n_1 + n_2 + n_3 - K)$ degree of freedom.
(ii) e_1^2 is ss. residuals from 1st sample with $(n_1 - K)$ degrees of freedom.
(iii) e_2^2 is ss. residuals from 2nd sample with $(n_2 - K)$ degrees of freedom.
(iv) e_3^2 is ss. residuals from 3rd sample with $(n_3 - K)$ degrees of freedom.
(v) The degrees of freedom for the numerator of Equation (7) is derived as $[(n_1 + n_2 + n_3 - K) - (n_1 + n_2 + n_3 - 3K)] = 2K$.
(vi) The degrees of freedom for the denominator of Equation (7) is given by $[(n_1 - K) + (n_2 - K) + (n_3 - K)] = (n_1 + n_2 + n_3 - 3K)$.
4 Papanek ([48], p. 122, footnote 5).
5 See Maddala ([42], p. 201).
6 In fact, some authors would like to prefer the dummy variable test over the Chow test. For instance, Gujarathi [27] suggests using the dummy-variable method in preference to the Chow test, arguing that the Chow test might reject the hypothesis of stability but not let us know which particular coefficients are unstable, whereas the dummy-variable method will give us this information.
7 Papanek ([48], p. 124).
8 Galbraith ([19], pp. 30–33).

CHAPTER IX

1 For the use of these two terms, see Papanek [48].
2 On this subject, see Gupta [29, 30].
3 That aggregation bias can seriously distort signs and magnitudes of estimated coefficients is well known. For example, see Gupta [29, 30].
4 Papanek ([48], p. 124).
5 Countries whose actual growth rate is substantially higher than predicted growth rate.
6 Countries whose actual growth rate is substantially lower than predicted growth rate.
7 Two of those countries do not appear in our sample. They are: Taiwan and Zambia.

BIBLIOGRAPHY

[1] Adelman, Irma: 'An Econometric Analysis of Population Growth', *American Economic Review* (June 1963), 314–39.

[2] Ahmed, Nasim: 'A Note on the Haavelmo Hypothesis', *Review of Economics & Statistics* **53** (1971).

[3] Bacha, E. L.: 'Foreign Capital Inflow and the Output Growth Rate of the Recipient Country', *The Journal of Development Studies* **10**, Nos. 3/4 (1974).

[4] Becker, Gary S.: 'An Economic Analysis of Fertility', in *Demographic and Economic Change in Developed Countries*, Universities-National Bureau Conference Series 11, Princeton University Press, Princeton, N.J., 1960.

[5] Benham, Lee: 'The Labour Market for Registered Nurses: A Three Equation Model', *Review of Economics & Statistics* (August 1971), 246–52.

[6] Cain, Glen C.: *Married Women in the Labour Force: An Economic Analysis*, Chicago University Press, Chicago, 1966.

[7] Cain, G. C. and Weininger, A.: 'Economic Determinants of Fertility: Results from Cross-Sectional Aggregate Data', *Demography* (May 1973), 205–24.

[8] Chenery, H. B.: 'Patterns of Industrial Growth', *American Economic Review* **50** (1960), 624–54.

[9] Chenery, H. B. and Adelman, I.: 'Foreign Aid and Economic Development: The Case of Greece', *Review of Economies and Statistics* (Feb. 1966).

[10] Chenery, H. B. and Eckstein, P.: 'Development Alternatives for Latin America', *Journal of Political Economy* (August 1970), 966–1006.

[11] Chenery, H. B. and Strout, A.: 'Foreign Assistance and Economic Development', *American Economic Review* (Sept. 1966).

[12] Chow, G. C.: 'Tests of Equality between Subsets of Coefficients in Two Linear Regressions', *Econometrica* (1960), 591–605.

[13] Christian, Jones W. and Pagoulatos, E.: 'Foreign Capital, Domestic Finance and Saving in Developing Countries', *Economia Internationale* (Feb.–May 1976), 81–6.

[14] Clark, Colin: *The Conditions of Economic Progress*, Macmillan, London, 1957.

[15] Dacy, D.: 'Foreign Aid, Government Consumption, Saving and Growth in Less Developed Countries', *The Economic Journal* **85** (1975), 548–61.

[16] Enke, Stephen: 'Population Growth and Economic Growth', *The Public Interest* (1973), 86–96.

[17] Frank, A. G.: *Capitalism and Underdevelopment in Latin America*, Monthly Review Press, 1969.

[18] Galbraith, J. K.: *The Underdeveloped Country*, CBC Publication, Toronto, 1965, pp. 20–33.

[19] Galbraith, J. K.: 'The Causes of Poverty: A Classification', in *Economics, Peace and Laughter*, Houghton-Mifflin, Boston, 1971.

[20] Goldberger, A. S.: *Econometric Theory*, John Wiley & Sons, New York, 1964.

[21] Granger, C. W. J.: 'Investigating Causal Relations by Econometric Models and Cross-Spectral Methods', *Econometrica* (July 1969), 424–38.

[22] Gregory, P. R., Campbell, J. M., and Benjamin, C.: 'A Cost-Inclusive Simultaneous Equation Model of Birth Rates', *Econometrica* (July 1972), 681–88.

[23] Griffin, K. B.: 'Foreign Capital, Domestic Savings and Economic Development', *Bulletin of the Oxford University Institute of Economics and Statistics* **32** (1970), 99–112.

[24] Griffin, K. B.: 'The Role of Foreign Capital', in Griffin, K. B. (ed.), *Financing Development in Latin America*, Macmillan, 1971, pp. 225–44.

[25] Griffin, K. B. and Enos, J. L.: 'Foreign Assistance: Objectives and Consequences', *Economic Development and Cultural Change* **18** (1970), 313–27.

[26] Grinols, E. and Bhagwati, J. N.: 'Foreign Capital, Savings and Dependence', *Review of Economics and Statistics* **58** (1976), 416–24.

[27] Gujarathi, D.: 'Use of Dummy Variables in Testing for Equality between Sets of Coefficients in Two Linear Regressions – A Note', *American Statistician* (February, 1970).

[28] Gualti, U.: 'Effects of Capital Imports on Savings and Growth in Less Developed Countries', *Economic Inquiry* **16** (1978), 563–69.

[29] Gupta, K. L.: *Aggregation in Economics*, Rotterdam University Press, Rotterdam, 1969.

[30] Gupta, K. L.: 'Aggregation in Linear Economic Models', *International Economic Review* **12** (1971), 293–305.

[31] Gupta, K. L.: 'Dependency Rates and Savings Rates', *American Economic Review* (June 1971), 469–71.

[32] Gupta, K. L.: 'Foreign Capital and Domestic Savings: A Test of Haavelmo's Hypothesis with Cross-Country Data: A Comment', *Review of Economics and Statistics* (May 1970), 214–16.

[33] Gupta, K. L.: 'Foreign Capital Inflows, Dependency Burden and Saving Rates in Developing Countries: A Simultaneous Equation Model', *Kyklos* **28** (1975), 358–74.

[34] Gupta, K. L.: 'Foreign Capital Inflows and Output Growth Rate: A Reformulation', *Journal of Development Studies* **XIII** (1976), 111–13.

[35] Haavelmo, Trygve: Comment on Leantief, Wassily, 'The Rates of Long-Run Economic Growth and Capital Transfer from Developed to Underdeveloped Areas', Study Week on *The Econometric Approach to Development Planning* (Oct. 7–13, 1963), North Holland Publishing Company, Amsterdam, 1965.

[36] Hirschman, A. O.: *The Strategy of Economic Development*, New Haven, Yale University Press, 1958.

[37] Houthakker, H. S.: 'On Some Determinants of Savings in Developed and Underdeveloped Countries', in E. A. G. Robinson (ed.), *Problems in Economic Development*, New York, Macmillan and Company, 1965.

[38] Kim, Y. C.: 'Sectoral Output-Capital Ratios and Levels of Economic Development: A Cross-Section Comparison of the Manufacturing Industry', *Review of Economics and Statistics* **51** (1969), 453–58.

[39] Kuznets, S.: *Modern Economic Growth*, Yale University Press, New Haven, 1966.

[40] Landau, L.: 'Determinants of Savings in Latin America', *Project for Quantitative Research on Economic Development*, Harvard University, 1966.

[41] Leff, N. H.: 'Dependency Rates and Savings Rates', *American Economic Review* **59** (1969), 886–96.

[42] Maddala, G. S.: *Econometrics*, McGraw Hill Book Company, New York, 1977.

[43] Mikesell, R. F. and J. E. Zinser: 'The Nature of the Savings Function in Developing Countries: A Survey of the Theoretical and Empirical Literature', *Journal of Economic Literature* (March 1973), 1–26.

[44] Mincer, Jacob: 'Market Prices, Opportunity Cost and Income Effects', in *Measurement in Economics*, Stanford, Stanford University Press, 1963.

[45] Modigliani, F.: 'The Life Cycle Hypothesis of Savings, the Demand for Wealth and the Supply of Capital', paper presented to the Rome Congress of the Econometric Society, 1965.

[46] Okun, B.: 'The Birth Rates and Economic Development: A Comment', *Econometrica* **33** (1965).

[47] Papanek, G. F.: 'The Effect of Aid and Other Resource Transfers on Savings and Growth in Less Developed Countries', *Economic Journal* **82** (1972), 934–50.

[48] Papanek, G. F.: 'Aid, Foreign Private Investment, Savings and Growth in Less Developed Countries', *Journal of Political Economy* **81** (1973), 120–30.

[49] Rahman, M. A.: 'Foreign Capital and Domestic Savings: A Test of Haavelmo's Hypothesis with Cross-Country Data', *Review of Economics and Statistics* **50** (1968), 137–38.

[50] Ram, R.: 'Foreign Capital, Savings and Economic Growth: An Agnostic Note', *Economic Inquiry* **18** (1980), 514–18.

[51] Rao, C. R.: *Advanced Statistical Methods in Biometric Research*, John Wiley & Sons, Inc., New York, 1952.

[52] Robinson, S.: 'Sources of Growth in Less Developed Countries: A Cross-Section Study', *Quarterly Journal of Economics* **85** (1971), 391–408.

[53] Rosenstein-Rodan, P. N.: 'International Aid for Underdeveloped Countries', *Review of Economics and Statistics* **43** (1961), 107–38.

[54] Schultz, P. T.: 'An Economic Model of Family Planning and Fertility', *Journal of Political Economy* **77** (1969), 153–180.

[55] Singh, S. K. (ed.): *Development Economics: Theory and Findings*, Heath, Lexington, Mass., 1972.

[56] Snyder, D. W.: 'Econometric Studies of Household Saving Behaviour in Developing Countries: A Survey', *Journal of Development Studies* **X** (1974), 139–53.

[57] Stewart, F.: 'Foreign Capital, Domestic Savings and Economic Development: Comment', *Bulletin of Oxford University Institute of Economics and Statistics* **33** (1971), 138–49.

[58] Stoneman, C.: 'Foreign Capital and Economic Growth', *World Development* **3** (1975), 11–26.

[59] Strout, A.: 'Korea's Use of Foreign and Domestic Resources: A Cross-Country Comparison', in I. Adelman (ed.): *Practical Approaches to Development Planning: Korea's Second Five Year Plan*, John Hopkins University Press, Baltimore, 1969.

[60] Swamy, S.: 'A Dynamic, Personal, Savings Function and Its Long-Run Implications', *Review of Economics and Statistics* (February 1968), 111–116.

[61] Todaro, M. P.: *Economic Development in the Third World*, 2nd Edition, Longman, New York, 1981.

[62] United Nations, Department of Social and Economic Affairs: 'Demographic Aspects of Manpower, Report I: Sex and Age Patterns of Participation in Economic Activities', *Population Studies*, No. 33, New York, 1962.

[63] Voivodas, C. S.: 'Exports, Foreign Capital Inflows and Economic Growth', *Journal of International Economics* **3** (1973), 337–49.

[64] Warren, B.: 'Imperialism and Capitalist Industrialization', *New Left Review*, No. 81 (1973), 3–44.

[65] Wasow, B.: 'Saving and Dependence with Externally Financed Growth', *Review of Economics and Statistics* **61** (1979), 150–54.

[66] Weisskoff, T. E.: 'An Econometric Test of Alternative Constraints on the Growth of Underdeveloped Countries', *Review of Economics and Statistics* **54**, No. 1, Part II (1972), 67–78.

[67] Weisskoff, T. E.: 'The Impact of Foreign Capital Inflow on Domestic Savings in Underdeveloped Countries', *Journal of International Economics* **2** (1972), 25–38.

INDEX

GPSR Compliance

The European Union's (EU) General Product Safety Regulation (GPSR) is a set of rules that requires consumer products to be safe and our obligations to ensure this.

If you have any concerns about our products, you can contact us on ProductSafety@springernature.com

In case Publisher is established outside the EU, the EU authorized representative is:

Springer Nature Customer Service Center GmbH
Europaplatz 3
69115 Heidelberg, Germany

Batch number: 10823811

Printed by Printforce, the Netherlands